Tackling Numeracy Issues
Book 7

Improving the plenary session Years 5 and 6

Caroline Clissold

A *Questions* book for teachers

Tackling Numeracy Issues
Book 7

Improving the plenary session
Years 5 and 6

Caroline Clissold

The *Questions* Publishing Company Limited
Birmingham
2002

The Questions Publishing Company Ltd
Leonard House, 321 Bradford Street, Digbeth, Birmingham B5 6ET

© The Questions Publishing Company Ltd 2002

First published in 2002

ISBN: 1-84190-078-8

Design and incidental illustration by Ivan Morison
Cover by Martin Cater

Printed in the UK

Also available from the Questions Publishing Company Limited:

Book 1 *Fractions and Decimals, Key Stage 1*
ISBN: 1-84190-079-6

Book 2 *Fractions, Decimals and Percentages, Key Stage 2*
ISBN: 1-84190-047-8

Book 3 *Fractions, Decimals, Percentages, Ratio and Proportion, Key Stage 2, Years 5 and 6*
ISBN: 1-84190-048-6

Book 4 *Solving Maths Word Problems*
ISBN: 1-84190-052-4

Book 5 *Improving the Plenary Session, Key Stage 1, Years 1 and 2*
ISBN: 1-84190-053-2

Book 6 *Improving the Plenary Session, Key Stage 2, Years 3 and 4*
ISBN: 1-84190-077-X

Contents

Introduction

According to Ofsted's report *The National Numeracy Strategy: An Interim Evaluation by HMI*, the plenary is the 'least successful element of the daily Maths lesson'. HMI stated that a typical problem was 'poor time management in the other elements of the lesson which meant that the time originally allocated to the plenary was lost.' The report stressed that the best plenary sessions are used to 'draw together the key ideas of the lesson, reinforce teaching points made earlier, assess what has been understood and correct errors and misconceptions.'

The plenary is designed to round off the maths lesson, with the class coming together as a whole. It should take between 10 and 15 minutes. Initially, you may have to make a big effort to make adequate time for a plenary. However, it soon becomes second nature.

This book focuses on how to improve the plenary part of your numeracy lessons. It gives basic lesson ideas, based on objectives from the National Numeracy Strategy's Framework for Teaching Mathematics. These will need developing and differentiating to suit your particular class. Each lesson idea comes with detailed suggestions for a suitable plenary session.

There are many ways in which the plenary part of the maths lesson can be executed. Here are some suggestions, most of which will be expanded on in this book:

- ✪ Ask the children to present and explain their work.
- ✪ Celebrate success in the children's work.
- ✪ Discuss what was the easiest/hardest/most enjoyable part of the lesson.
- ✪ Make a note of any successes and/or misconceptions to be dealt with at the time or during the next lesson. If common misconceptions are discovered during the lesson, it might be helpful to shorten the lesson and increase the plenary time to deal with these.
- ✪ Mark a written exercise done individually during the lesson, so that you can question the children appropriately and assess their work.
- ✪ Discuss and compare the efficiency of children's methods of working out a calculation.
- ✪ Help the children to generalise a rule from examples generated by different groups.
- ✪ Draw together what has been learned; reflect on what was important in the lesson; summarise key facts, ideas and vocabulary and what needs to be remembered.
- ✪ Play a fun game relevant to the maths learnt during the lesson.
- ✪ At the end of a unit of work, draw together what has been learnt over a series of lessons.
- ✪ Link skills that have been learned to problem solving within a context relevant to the children.
- ✪ Discuss what pupils will do next as a progression from the present lesson.
- ✪ Consolidate and develop what has been learnt. For example, if the lesson was about numbers on a number square, review the objectives and develop them further, extending the activity with larger numbers.
- ✪ Make links to work in other maths topics or other subjects.
- ✪ Set homework or a challenge to be done out of class.

It must be stressed that each activity needs to be related to the objective of the lesson.

Variety is essential. The same type of plenary will soon become tedious for both yourself and the children. It is therefore important that different aspects are covered during each week. All sessions, of course, will involve assessment of varying degrees.

There are a few important things to remember:

- ✪ Have a clear plan in mind of what you want to achieve during the plenary.
- ✪ Make sure you leave enough time for it.
- ✪ Ensure that the children know if they are to present something during the plenary, so that they can prepare for it.
- ✪ At the end of the plenary make a general evaluation of the lesson's success and how the children have worked.
- ✪ Have a definite routine at the end of a lesson to mark its finish, this is particularly relevant for the younger children.

Topics and objectives

Chapter 1 Presentation of the children's work

Ideas for plenary sessions that give selected groups of children opportunities for showing and explaining their work to the rest of the class, based on lesson ideas which have the following objectives:

Year 5 objectives:

Multiply and divide whole numbers, then decimals, by 10, 100, 1000

Recognise and extend number sequences formed by counting on and back in steps of any size

Solve simple problems involving ratio

Recognise the equivalences between fractions and percentages

Use related facts and doubling and halving

Develop calculator skills and use a calculator effectively

Know and use relationships between familiar units

Recognise positions and directions

Year 6 objectives:

Addition of two decimal numbers to make a whole integer

Recognise multiples and know some tests of divisibility

Change fractions to decimals and order them

Solve simple problems involving ratio and proportion

Decide what to do after division, and round up and down accordingly

Recognise the operation represented by §

Solve 'story' problems involving metric and imperial measurements

Find the mode, range, mean and median of a set of data

Chapter 2 Progression — where are we going next?

Ideas for plenary sessions which will highlight where the work the children have been doing will lead for the next lesson, based on lesson ideas which have the following objectives:

Year 5 objectives:

Make and justify estimates and approximations of numbers

Recognise and order negative numbers in temperature

Recognise the rules of divisibility of 100, 10, 2, 4, 5

Round decimal fractions to the nearest whole number or tenth

Find out what to add to a decimal number with units and tenths to make the next higher whole number

Choose and use appropriate number operations and calculation methods to solve problems

Investigate a general statement about angles.

Read the time to the minute on a 24 hour digital clock

Year 6 objectives:
Multiply and divide whole numbers and decimals by 10, 100 or 1000
Recognise and extend number sequences by finding and continuing a pattern
Understand percentages as the number of parts in every hundred, recognise the equivalence between percentages and fractions and decimals
Understand and use when appropriate the principles of the distributive law of multiplication
Develop and refine written methods for the division of whole numbers
Record readings from scales to a suitable degree of accuracy
Measure and calculate the area of compound shapes using the formula for finding the area of a rectangle
Read and plot points using co-ordinates beyond the first quadrant

Chapter 3 Links to other maths topics and curriculum areas

Numeracy and literacy:	Problem solving
	Creative/factual writing
	Vocabulary
	Sound blends
Numeracy and science:	Keeping Healthy
	Earth, Sun and Moon
	How We See Things
	Forces in Action
Numeracy and history:	How has life in Britain changed since 1948
	What were the effects of Tudor exploration?
Numeracy and geography:	Should the High Street be closed to traffic?
	Geography and Numbers
Numeracy and art:	Talking Textiles
Numeracy and PE	
Other areas of maths	

Chapter 4 Problem solving and games
Visualising
Acting out
Making up problems
Two-step problems
Games

Chapter 1

Presentation and explanation of the children's work

When the National Numeracy Strategy was first put into place in primary schools, many teachers felt that this aspect of the lesson was not really important. In a lot of cases there was no time left for it at the end of the lesson, or if there was, the plenary consisted of a quick 'let's see what this group have done today' or the show and tell approach.

In my observations of lessons I still meet with teachers who say such things as:
"I don't want to stop the children when they are working so hard."
"Oh dear, I ran out of time."
"I'm not very good at plenaries, so I tend not to do them."
Happily, I meet far more teachers these days who are increasingly seeing the importance and value of the plenary part of the lesson, and use it confidently with a valid purpose.

At the beginning of the plenary it is always important to refer to the objectives of the lesson. If you are using the explaining and presenting approach, the selected group of children/pairs/individuals will need to be able to tell the other children in the class what they have been doing, how it has helped them understand or has reinforced the objectives from the main teaching activity and whether they feel they have been successful.

It can be counter productive to ask the children to explain what they have been doing and how they got on during the plenary without prior warning. Doing so can cause embarrassment and anxiety in some children. It can also lack focus and quite frankly be a waste of ten minutes. The children need to be told in advance that they will be asked to talk about their work and how it has helped them achieve the lesson objectives, so that they can be prepared.

If you have a teaching assistant, it might be worth considering asking them to help the group they are working with to plan their plenary activity The teaching assistant does not necessarily need to work with the less able group always. Remember that it is the teacher's responsibility to teach that group at least once or twice a week. On these occasions you might ask your assistant to work with other children to help them with their presentation skills. Some children will welcome this help, as presenting and explaining work without a real focus can be very daunting to some, even the most able.

It is helpful to have a selection of appropriate questions that you might ask the children during the plenary, for example:

- ✪ What activity have you been doing during this session?
- ✪ Can you explain why you have been doing this?
- ✪ Has it helped you achieve the objectives?
- ✪ What do you know now that you didn't before?

Year 5

1. Multiplying and dividing

> **Objective:** Multiply and divide whole numbers, then decimals, by 10, 100, 1000
> **Strand:** Numbers and the number system
> **Topic:** Place value (whole numbers and decimals)

Paired activity
Writing a single digit integer and x and ÷ it by 10, 100, 1000, and explaining what is happening.

Use some of the digit cards on photocopiable sheet 1 – one digit, three zeros and a decimal point – for a class demonstration. Give one child the digit say, 6, three others the zeros and a fifth the decimal point. Ask the child with the 6 to stand at the front of the room. Ask the children what happens when you multiply it by 10, i.e. it gets 10 times bigger. Do this by asking a child with a zero to make 60. Ask what happens when you multiply by 100, i.e. it get 100 times bigger. Ask two children with zeros to make 600. Do the same for 1000. Ask the children what happens if you divide 6 by 10, i.e. it gets 10 times smaller. Ask the child with the decimal point to help to make 0.6. Repeat for ÷ by 100 and 1000. Make sure the child with the decimal point does not move and the others move around him/her.
Model the paired activity by writing a number on the board and multiplying and dividing it by 10, 100 and 1000:

x 1000	6000
x 100	600
x 10	60
	6
÷ 10	0.6
÷ 100	0.06
÷ 1000	0.006

Ask the pairs of children to use their digit cards to choose random single digit numbers and repeat the activity you modelled.
Ask the pairs of children to progress to picking two digit cards to make up a two-digit number and, if time, a three-digit number.

Plenary
Refer to the objectives! Invite some of the pairs of children to demonstrate their work with two-digit numbers. Ask them to choose some of the others in the class to help them to demonstrate x and ÷ of three-digit numbers as you did, using their digit cards and your zeros and decimal point.

2. Number sequences

> **Objective:** Recognise and extend number sequences formed by counting on and back in steps of any size
> **Strand:** Numbers and the number system
> **Topic:** Properties of numbers and the number system

Paired activity
Using the constant function on a calculator to generate multiples of any number.

Use an OHP calculator to demonstrate this activity. Type in a function without the children seeing, keep pressing = and ask the children what is happening. Begin with an easy example and then do a few more complicated ones, for example:

Type in 3 + = 0, then, in front of the children =, =, =, etc. They should see this sequence: 3, 6, 9, 12, 15, 18, and so on.
Type: 9 - = 23 = = = =, etc. They should see: 23, 14, 5, -4, -13, -22, and so on.
Tell the children how to do this. For their paired activity give them instruction cards.
One of the pair needs to follow the instructions, the other needs to try and work out the sequence. See photocopiable sheet 2. Once they have completed these they could make up their own.

Plenary
Refer to the objectives! Ask one or two of the pairs to demonstrate what they did using the OHP and OHP calculator, this time pretending that the rest of the class is their partner.

3. Ratio

> **Objective:** Solve simple problems involving ratio
> **Strand:** Numbers and the number system
> **Topic:** Solve simple problems involving ratio and proportion

Paired activity
Mixing two different coloured paints to different ratios.

Explain the concept of ratio; that it is one part of something to another part of something else. Use ten OHP counters of two different colours and an OHP to make this clear:

Example

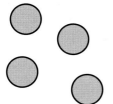
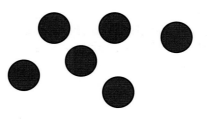

Explain that there are ten counters: four are green and six are blue. For every four green counters there are six blue ones. This is a ratio and can be written 4:6.

Demonstrate again using paint, involving the children in this, e.g. one teaspoon of blue and four of yellow, one teaspoon of blue and two of yellow. Explain the ratio as before. You will end up with different shades of green. Paint them on paper so that the children can see the effect of the different ratios.

Give the groups of children access to some red and yellow paints, paintbrushes, spoons and paper. As a group, they need to decide which child will mix the paints to which ratio, e.g. child 1 may mix the paints to a ratio of one spoon of red to two of yellow, child 2 might choose two of red to one of yellow. After each child has decided and mixed their paint, they need to make a splodge of it on their paper and label the ratio. After this, encourage the children to look at each others 'splodges' and order the shades from lightest to darkest. Ask the children to be prepared to show the others what they have done during the plenary session.

Plenary
Refer to the objectives! Ask selected groups to show their 'splodges'. Ask the rest of the class to order their paintings and guess what ratios they had used. The groups then need to tell the class if their guesses were correct or not. Order the ratios on a number line on the board from lightest to darkest.

4. Fractions and percentages

> **Objective:** Recognise the equivalences between fractions and percentages
> **Strand:** Numbers and the number system
> **Topic:** Fractions, decimals and percentages

Paired activity
Colouring percentages and linking them to equivalent fractions.

Begin by demonstrating the fact that a percentage is a fraction of 100, using a percentage square and strips of card to cover the whole, half, quarter, fifth, tenth, twentieth and hundredth. Use the percentage square on photocopiable sheet 3.

Cover up 50% with the $\frac{1}{2}$ card. Ask what fraction has been covered: look for the answers $\frac{50}{100}$ and $\frac{1}{2}$. Repeat with the quarter piece, fifth piece, tenth piece, etc. in the same way. Fill in a table on the board similar to the following:

Percentage	Fraction	Fraction
50%	$\frac{50}{100}$	$\frac{1}{2}$
25%	$\frac{25}{100}$	$\frac{1}{4}$
20%	$\frac{20}{100}$	$\frac{1}{5}$
10%	$\frac{10}{100}$	$\frac{1}{10}$

Ask the children in pairs to complete the activity on photocopiable sheet 3.

Plenary
Refer to the objectives! Ask a 'selected' pair of children to demonstrate their work using your percentage square and centimetre cubes to cover the squares they coloured in. They need to explain clearly and in detail, how they worked out the fractions from the percentages covered.

5. Mental calculation

Objective: Use related facts and doubling and halving
Strand: Calculations
Topic: Mental calculation strategies (x and ÷)

Group activity
Answering calculations mentally, using known facts and adapting them.

Write some calculations on the board and ask the children which they think is the quickest way to answer them, for example:

36 x 50   (multiply by 100 and halve)
9 x 16   (9 x 8 and double)
43 x 20   (multiply by 10 and double)
18 x 2.5   (multiply by 10 and halve and halve again)

Split the class into groups of three or four. This activity is a race game. Give each group a pile of calculation cards. When you say 'go', give the children five minutes to answer as many calculations as possible.

Example

14 x 50	**42 x 20**	**8 x 16**
23 x 20	**14 x 16**	**56 x 50**

They must record the answer and the strategy they used.

Plenary
Refer to the objectives! Ask the winning group to come to the front and explain to the rest of the class the strategies they used to answer their calculations. Invite any of the other children to put forward a strategy that they think is more efficient if they can think of one.

6. Calculator skills

Objective: Develop calculator skills and use a calculator effectively
Strand: Calculations
Topic: Using a calculator

Group activity
Selecting the correct key sequences to carry out calculations involving more than one step, such as 8 x (37 + 58).

Begin by writing on the board: 6 x 45 – 19. Ask the children to work this out using a calculator. They will probably answer 251. Give them two problems relating to the calculation, for example:

There were six children. Each had 45 alien stickers but one of them lost 19 of his. *How many alien stickers did they have altogether?*

Tina had 45 marbles. She gave 19 to a friend. Her brother gave her his collection which meant she now had six times as many. *How many marbles does she have now?*

Ask the children which problem their answer of 251 goes with. (The first one.) Then ask them what they would have to do to get the answer to the other problem. (45 – 19 x 6 which equals 156.)

Introduce the idea of putting the numbers in the same order but using brackets to signify the part of the calculation that needs to be done first: (6 x 45) – 9 and 6 x (45 – 19).

Match them with the problems.

For the group activity, give the children some calculations. For each of the calculations put brackets around different numbers. Ask the children to solve them using a calculator and make up a problem for each.

Example

(45 ÷ 5) x 2	45 ÷ (5 x 2)
Answer: 18	**Answer:** 4.5
Problem:	**Problem:**

Plenary

Refer to the objectives! Ask one of the groups to read their problems and to choose a class member to write the sums on the board with the numbers in the same order, using brackets for one of them.

7. Measuring

> **Objective:** Know and use relationships between familiar units
> **Strand:** Measures
> **Topic:** Length, mass and capacity

Paired activity

Recognising and recording lengths in different ways.

Begin by asking the children to build numbers using their digit cards and explain what each digit represents, e.g. 45.5, 58.25. Link this to length by first talking about, and then demonstrating using rulers and a metre stick, how many centimetres there are in a metre and how measurements that are whole metres and centimetres can be written, e.g. 1 whole metre and 50 centimetres can be written as 1.50m.

Each child will need a 'show me strip' (a piece of card split into 10 equal pieces, see photocopiable sheet 4 for examples) and paper clip. Call out some lengths for them to show on the strip, e.g. if one end of the strip is 1 and the other is 2, put the paper clip on 1.5m, 1.2m, 1.25m, 1m 30cms, 1m 70cm.

Give the children photocopiable sheet 4. Tell them to plot the measurements on the show me strips.

Example

2m 20cms

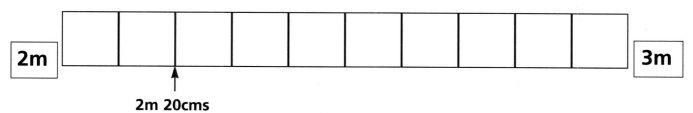

2m 20cms

Plenary

Refer to the objectives! Ask 'selected' pairs of children to demonstrate using a large 'show me' strip where they put the different lengths they were working on.

8. Position and direction

> **Objective:** Recognise positions and directions
> **Strand:** Shape and space
> **Topic:** Position and direction

Paired activity

Understanding and using the terms perpendicular, parallel and diagonal.

Show some shapes with lines drawn on. Ask the children to name the shapes and tell you what the dotted lines are called and why.

Examples

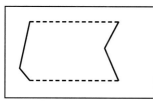

Name: Hexagon because it's got six sides.
Dotted lines: Parallel because they will stay the same distance apart along their whole length and never meet.

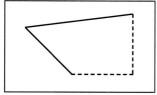

Name: Quadrilateral because it's got six sides.
Dotted lines: Perpendicular because they are at right angles to each other.

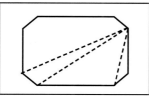

Name: Octagon because it's got eight sides.
Dotted lines: Diagonal because they are straight lines from a vertex to another vertex which is not next to it.

Ask groups of children to make shape posters filled with shapes that have parallel, perpendicular and diagonal lines. Ask them to draw the special lines in another colour.

Plenary
Refer to the objectives! Invite groups to describe the shapes on their posters and the lines that are being focused on. They need to explain what makes them what they are.

Year 6

9. Place value

> **Objective:** Addition of two decimal numbers to make a whole integer
> **Strand:** Numbers and the Number System
> **Topic:** Place value (whole numbers and decimals)

Paired activity
Pairing decimal numbers or sets of three decimal numbers to make a whole number.

Use decimal digit cards, one set per child or pair. Tell the children that you need to make one whole number. You have 0.4. Ask them to show you how much more you need to make a whole. Repeat a few times. Tell them that you need 5 and have 2.7. Ask them to show you how much more you need. Repeat using different whole numbers.
Try hundredths: you need one whole number and only have 0.09. How much more?
Give each of the pairs of children a pile of cards with a decimal number and the whole number the children need to make. Their task is to calculate how much more is needed and record.

Examples

6.7 Make 10	1.4 Make 5	26.6 Make 30	1.05 Make 2	2.17 Make 4

Plenary
Refer to the objectives! Ask a few of the pairs to come to the front to demonstrate their work. They need to explain clearly their strategies for answering the calculations.

10. Multiples and divisibility

> **Objective:** Recognise multiples and know some tests of divisibility
> **Strand:** Numbers and the number system
> **Topic:** Properties of numbers and number sequences

Paired activity
Working with multiples of 3 and 9 and recognising their tests of divisibility.

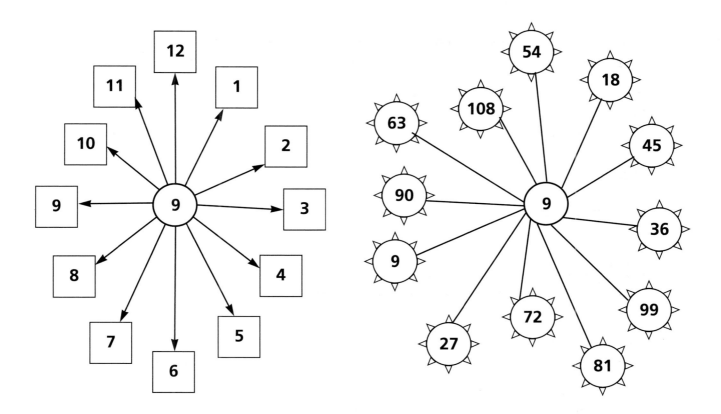

Rehearse the 9 x table using the clock chart shown above (point randomly to the numbers 1 to 12; the children need to multiply that number by 9 and call out the answer).

Show the 'spider' chart and ask the children what they notice about the digits that make up the answers to this table. Aim towards the idea that adding the digits will always give 9. Talk about the usefulness of this 'trick' to help them know if a number is divisible by 9. Ask the children to say a two-digit number, e.g. 34, you reply with 7; 26, you reply 8; 72, you reply 9. Repeat several times. Invite the children to write some numbers on the board and you write the answers as before. This time use examples like this: 56 … 11… 2; 79 …16 …7. Find out if they can see a pattern in their numbers and your answers. Try some three-digit numbers.

Explain that this is a good method of finding out if a number is divisible by 3, 6, 9.

Give pairs of children photocopiable sheet 5.

Plenary

Refer to the objectives! Discuss the work with the children. Invite some pairs to come to the front and write a few of their two- or three-digit numbers on the board. Ask the rest of the class to tell them if they are divisible by 3 or 9, by using the 'add the digit' rule.

11. Fractions and decimals

> **Objective:** Change fractions to decimals and order them
> **Strand:** Numbers and the number system
> **Topic:** Fractions

Paired activity

Ordering decimals and fractions on a number line.

Give each child a 'show me' strip (see example on page 7). Pretend one end is 0 and the other is 1 whole. Ask them to show you where $^1/_{10}$ would be, $^1/_2$, $^1/_4$, $^2/_5$, $^7/_{10}$ etc. Discuss tenths as decimals – one tenth is the same as 0.1, five tenths 0.5 etc. Ask the children to show you where various decimals are on their 'show me' strips. Link other fractions to decimals e.g. $^1/_4$, $^3/_4$, $^1/_8$. Use your 'show me' strips to find the fractions and decimals below.

$^1/_{10}$ $^3/_{10}$ $^7/_{10}$ $^1/_2$ $^9/_{10}$ $^1/_4$ $^3/_4$ **0.2 0.5 0.8 0.25 0.1 0.7 0.125**

Once you have put the paper clip in the right place, make a number line with the fractions on the top and the decimals on the bottom. Don't forget to write the equivalents on the opposite part of the line.

Plenary
Refer to the objectives! Ask a pair of children to demonstrate the work they have been doing by drawing a number line on the board and explaining clearly how they worked out where to put the different numbers. Finish by asking the class to add other numbers to the line the pair started, e.g. 0.625, $^4/_5$, and to convert them to either decimals or fractions

12. Ratio and proportion

Objective: Solve simple problems involving ratio and proportion
Strand: Numbers and the number system
Topic: Ratio and proportion

Group activity
Reducing heights to a ratio that can be drawn on paper.

Show a picture of a child, preferably a photograph. Ask the children what is the difference between the picture and a real child. Expect all kinds of answers, accept them but lead towards the size aspect. Explain that the child is in proportion but smaller and what has been done to make them smaller.
Choose some children to help you. Tell the class that you want to make a drawing of each child, to show how tall they are, but you only have a piece of A3 paper. Ask for suggestions of how to do this. Hopefully, someone may suggest something similar to this: for every 10cms tall that they are draw 1cm. If no-one does, make that suggestion yourself. Measure your helpers. Write their heights on the board and convert them to a ratio of 1cm for every 10cms, so if one of your helpers is 1m 45cms tall, their representation on paper will be 14.5cms.
Ask some children to draw the heights you have converted and order them from tallest to shortest. Do the same with the children and see if the two are comparable.
Give small groups of the children the activity on photocopiable sheet 6.
After completing this activity, draw pairs of lines to represent each building at a ratio of 1cm:10m and 1cm:100m. Ask the children what they notice about the pairs of lines.

Plenary
Refer to the objectives! Ask one of the groups of children to explain how they worked out their ratios 1cm:10m and 1cm:100m. They need to comment about the effect of doing this and how it is helpful to be able to do so. They also need to be able to explain the relationship between the two different ratios they have worked out.

13. Rounding up

> **Objective:** Decide what to do after division, and round up and down accordingly
> **Strand:** Calculations
> **Topic:** Understanding division

Paired activity
Making sensible decisions about rounding up or down according to the context of the question.

Examples
I have 5m of rope. I need lengths of 865cm.
How many lengths can I cut off?
5000 ÷ 865 = 5. 780. I can cut off five lengths.

5000 football fans have tickets for a match. Each stand seats 865 people.
How many stands will house the fans?
5000 ÷ 865 = 5.780. They need six stands.

Give similar problems to the pairs of children. Allow them to use calculators.

Plenary
Refer to the objectives! Ask several pairs to help in this plenary. Each pair should explain one of the problems each: what they needed to find out, how they worked out the answer and finally how they decided whether to round up or down. Discuss with the whole class whether their answer makes sense or not.

14. Choosing the right operation

> **Objective:** Recognise the operation represented by □
> **Strand:** Solving problems
> **Topic:** Making decisions

Paired activity
Solving calculations with a symbol to signify the operation needed.

Write some examples of the type of calculations you want the children to work on, on the board. Discuss with them, how they will solve them.

Examples
469 □ 83 = 5.65	469 □ 83 = 552
469 □ 83 = 386	469 □ 83 = 38927

First of all they need to make a sensible prediction about what the signs should be, judging by the answer.
They can check using a calculator.
Give the pairs of children sets of four calculations similar to those demonstrated and ask them to make sensible predictions and then check using a calculator.

Plenary
Refer to the objectives! Choose several volunteers to explain to everyone how they made their predictions and then how they checked whether they were correct. Ask them to tell the children how successful their predictions were and whether they found this easy to do or not.

15. Measures

Objective: Solve 'story' problems involving metric and imperial measurements
Strand: Solving problems
Topic: Problems involving measures

Group activity
Converting recipes from Imperial measures to metric.

Discuss the use of gallons and pints, pounds and ounces. Compare them to metric measures:
1.75 pints is approximately 1 litre
1 pound is approximately 0.45 kg
16 ounces (oz) = 1 pound (lb)
Work through a recipe, converting Imperial measures to metric, using a calculator.

Example

Ingredients	Imperial measures	Metric measures
Water	Half a pint	
Butter	3oz	
Sugar	4oz	
Flour	10oz	
Almond essence	1 teaspoon	
Eggs	2	

Give groups of children similar recipes to convert using calculators.

Plenary
Refer to the objectives! Ask a group of children to come to the front of the class and explain to the rest of the children how they made their conversions. If possible, it would be a good idea to let the children use an OHP calculator and an OHP, as the conversions can be quite complicated and it would be helpful for everyone to see the steps that the group goes through.

16. Mode, range, mean and median

Objective: Find the mode, range, mean and median of a set of data
Strand: Handling data
Topic: Organising and interpreting data

Paired activity
Analysing and interpreting data from a graph, finding the mode, range, mean and median.

Remind the children of the five aspects of handling data:

- ✪ Specifying the problem – formulating questions in terms of the data that is needed and the type of inferences that can be made from them.
- ✪ Planning – deciding what data needs collecting, including sample size and data format and what statistical analysis needs to be carried out.
- ✪ Collecting data – from a variety of appropriate sources including experiments, surveys and primary and secondary data.
- ✪ Processing and representing – including lists, tables and charts.
- ✪ Interpreting and discussion – relating the summarised data to the initial question.

Make up a problem, e.g. How can we find last week's spelling test scores for the whole of Year 6 and work out what the mode, range, mean and median of the scores are?
Follow the other aspects of the lesson – plan, collect data, represent the information.
For the small-group activity, ask the children to interpret the representation of the data, making up as many facts as possible from it. Ask them to work out what the mode, range, mean (calculator use is permissible) and median data are and expect them to be able to tell you what they are and why they might be useful.

Plenary
Refer to the objectives! Choose one group to tell everyone the facts that they came up with. After they have done this, invite others to add to their observations if they can. Then ask the group to tell everyone how they worked out the mode (the most common score), the range (from lowest to highest), the mean (the average) and the median (the middle score). Ask them to give suggestions as to why these pieces of information could be useful to the teacher.

Photocopiable Sheet 1
Multiplying and dividing

1	2	3
4	5	6
7	8	9
0	0	0
0	0	.

Photocopiable Sheet 2
Number sequences

On your calculator type:
25 + = 0
Then keep typing =.
Ask your friend what the sequence is.

On your calculator type:
2 x = 2
Then keep typing =.
Ask your friend what the sequence is.

On your calculator type:
10 x = 10
Then keep typing =.
Ask your friend what the sequence is.

On your calculator type:
19 - = 75
Then keep typing =.
Ask your friend what the sequence is.

Photocopiable Sheet 3
Fractions and percentages

Colour:
25 squares red
10 squares blue
50 squares brown
1 square orange
5 squares yellow

1%	1%	1%	1%	1%	1%	1%	1%	1%	1%
1%	1%	1%	1%	1%	1%	1%	1%	1%	1%
1%	1%	1%	1%	1%	1%	1%	1%	1%	1%
1%	1%	1%	1%	1%	1%	1%	1%	1%	1%
1%	1%	1%	1%	1%	1%	1%	1%	1%	1%
1%	1%	1%	1%	1%	1%	1%	1%	1%	1%
1%	1%	1%	1%	1%	1%	1%	1%	1%	1%
1%	1%	1%	1%	1%	1%	1%	1%	1%	1%
1%	1%	1%	1%	1%	1%	1%	1%	1%	1%
1%	1%	1%	1%	1%	1%	1%	1%	1%	1%

Now fill in this table:

Colour	Number of squares	Percentage	Fraction
Red			
Blue			
Brown			
Orange			
Yellow			

Photocopiable Sheet 4
Measuring

1.5m

| 1m | | | | | | | | | | | 2m |

2m 75cms

3m 40cms

2.3m

6.85m

5.75m

Photocopiable Sheet 5
Multiples and divisibility

Write inside the pentagons 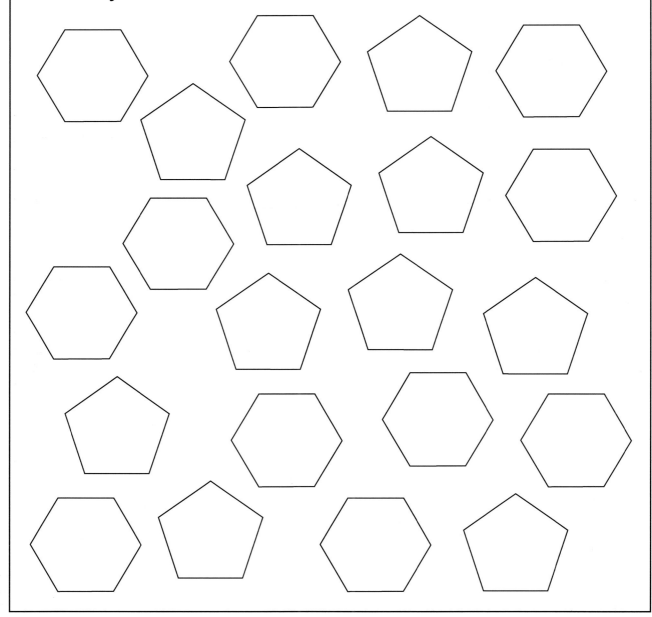 **some 2- or 3-digit numbers that can be divided by 3.**

Write indide the hexagons some 2- or 3-digit numbers that can be divided by 9.

Use the 'add the digit' rules.

Remember, they must add up to 9 to be divisable by 9, and 9 or 3 to be divisible by 3.

© The Questions Publishing Company Ltd

Photocopiable Sheet 6
Ratios

Building	Height	Ratio of 1cm:10m	Ratio of 1cm:100m
St. Paul's Cathedral	111m		
Big Ben	97m		
London Hilton	100m		
Blackpool Tower	158m		
Empire State Building	381m		
Bank of Manhattan	274m		
Fawley Power Station	198m		
Canary Wharf Tower	244m		

Work out the measurements of these buildings in centimetres at ratios of 1cm for every 10m and 1cm for every 100m

Chapter 2
Progression – where are we going next?

Put yourself inside the mind of a young child who has been asked to estimate a number of items. Their immediate reaction will probably be to think:

- ✪ I want to count them to find out exactly how many there are.
- ✪ I can count: why should I guess and maybe get it wrong?
- ✪ What is the point of estimating?
- ✪ I think I'll count and hope the teacher doesn't see me!

Does this sound familiar?

Estimating is a very good example of why it is important that the children know the purpose of what they are doing and where it will lead in the future. Estimating is a useful skill if the children need to know numbers and measurements in a practical context, for example:

- ✪ Will there be enough potatoes in this bag for our family to eat this Sunday?
- ✪ Will I have enough pennies to go to the shop to buy some sweets?

Estimating the answer first, answering and comparing the answer to the estimate is also important for calculation work. If they are close, the answer is likely to be correct and it will be worth a proper check.

This is the same in all areas of maths. It is important that the children know the 'whole picture' of what they are learning and why, so that they can see that it is relevant to them. Children always learn best if they can see why they are doing something. On occasions, during your plenary, tell the children how what they have learnt will help them during the next lesson.

This chapter aims to give lesson objectives from the NNS Framework for Teaching Mathematics, lesson ideas and a plenary outlining where the work the children have been doing will lead for the next lesson.

Remember to refer to the objective of the lesson taught initially and then inform the children of what they will be doing next time and why.

Year 5

1. Estimating proportions

> **Objective:** Make and justify estimates and approximations of numbers
> **Leading to:** Estimating a proportion
> **Strand:** Numbers and the number system
> **Topic:** Estimating (whole numbers)

Paired activity
Making different estimations of real things.

Begin by asking the children to make estimates of numbers of objects. Have a selection prepared: a string bag with cubes in it, a sliced loaf of bread, a plate with raisins on, etc. Ask the children to estimate how many cubes, slices of bread and raisins there are and explain how they made their estimate.
Give pairs of children estimation problems, such as:

✪ Estimate how many penny coins will make a straight line, 1 metre long. Now check.

✪ Estimate how many petals there are on these four daisies. Now check.

Plenary
Discuss the children's paired work. Ask them if their estimating got better the more they tried and how they made their estimates.
Tell them that during the next lesson they will be estimating proportions of items.
Give examples:
Show a piece of string and ask the children to estimate where to cut off one fifth.
Ask them how they made this estimate. Repeat with a different fraction.
Show the children a jar of dried peas; take some out. Ask them to estimate what proportion of the jar now contains peas. Repeat taking out another amount.

2. Negative numbers

> **Objective:** Recognise and order negative numbers in temperature
> **Leading to:** Using their knowledge to use negative numbers in other contexts
> **Strand:** Numbers and the number system
> **Topic:** Negative numbers

Paired activity
Recognising negative numbers on a thermometer.

Begin by discussing temperature and how it is measured. Talk about negative numbers and how cold it is when we can read them as a measurement on a thermometer. Look at a number line that goes into negative numbers. Ask the children such questions as "If we start on 4 and count back 10, what number are we on?". "Start at –8, count on 15, where are we now?"

Give the children photocopiable sheet 7 - the Thermometer Game:
  Each child throws three dice and using any of the four operations tries to make a
  number on the –10 to 10 thermometer number line, e.g. throw 6 3 5   6 + 3 = 9
  5 – 9 = - 4. If possible they then put a coloured counter in the shape beside the number.
  If it is not possible they miss a go. The winner is the child with the most counters on the
  thermometer.

Plenary
Tell the children that now they can read a thermometer, during their next lesson they will
be answering problems involving negative numbers in a different context. Give an example:
A diver has dived down into the water. He is at a depth of –30m. If he goes up 13m and
then down 5m, where is he? Invite one of the children to try to illustrate this on the board.

3. Divisibility

Objective: Recognise the rules of divisibility of 100, 10, 2, 4, 5
Leading to: Using their knowledge to work out that, for example, the year 2004 is a
leap year
Strand: Numbers and the number system
Topic: Properties of numbers

Paired activity
Sorting numbers into sets according to their divisibility.

Remind the children of the rules of divisibility:

100	if the last two digits are 00
10	if the last digit is 0
2	if its last digit is 0, 2, 4, 6 or 8
4	if the last two digits are divisible by 4
5	if the last digit is 0 or 5

Give the children some cards with numbers on and ask them to sort them using Venn
Diagrams into multiples using the rules of divisibility above.

Example

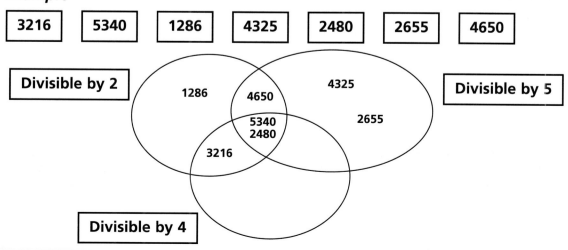

Plenary

Discuss with the children how they worked out which number should go where. Ask them what they noticed about the numbers that were divisible by 4.

Tell the children that they will be using this knowledge that they now have to work out other problems, for example that the year 2004 is a leap year because 2004 is divisible by 4 and every 4th year is a leap year.

4. Rounding decimals

Objective: Round decimal fractions to the nearest whole number or tenth
Leading to: Rounding up or down according to the context of a situation
Strand: Numbers and the number system
Topic: Fractions and decimals

Group activity

Rounding lengths to the nearest metre or tenth of a metre.

Discuss the concept of rounding with the children. Demonstrate by using a number line and markers. Place a marker on certain numbers. Ask the children to round various decimal numbers to the nearest whole number. Repeat to the nearest tenth.
Give the groups of children some number cards with lengths written on. The children need to pick a card, round it to what the instruction says and then record.

Example

6.7m Round to the nearest metre	8.29m Round to the nearest tenth of a metre
6.7m to the nearest metre is 7m.	8.29m to the nearest tenth of a metre is 8.3m.
9.1m Round to the nearest metre	2.87m Round to the nearest tenth of a metre
9.1m to the nearest metre is 9m.	2.87m to the nearest tenth of a metre is 2.9m.

Plenary

Ask one or two of the groups to feed back the work they have done. Tell the children that as they have done so well today, tomorrow they will be solving problems, thinking about rounding either up or down depending on the context of a question. Give a few examples:

The fabric shop sells material by the metre. I would like to make a pair of curtains. Each one will take 6.75m of material.
How many whole metres of material do I need to buy?
My friend estimated that she would need 0.60 metres of string to wrap her parcel.
How many metres would she need to wrap 13 parcels?
Boris' slug crawled about 0.07m per minute.
How many tenths of a metre would it be able to crawl over seven minutes?

5. Mental calculations

> **Objective:** Find out what to add to a decimal number with units and tenths to make the next higher whole number
> **Leading to:** Using their knowledge to find missing numbers in decimal number sentences
> **Strand:** Calculations
> **Topic:** Mental calculation strategies (+ and -)

Paired activity

Adding on decimals to make whole numbers.

Begin by giving each child a set of decimal digit cards, similar to the examples below. Tell them that you need 2 and that you have 1.7. Ask them to show you what you need to make 2. Tell them that you need 8 and have 7.7. Ask the children to show you what you need to make 8. Repeat several times.
Give the pairs of children a set of cards with numbers on and numbers to make, and ask them to record what they need to add onto the number to make the total required.

Examples

| **1.8** **make 4** | **3.2** **make 8** | **7.2** **make 12** |

Plenary

Discuss the work that the children have been doing. Ask a few pairs to show the others how they worked their problems out.
Tell the children that during the next lesson they will be learning to use this knowledge to find missing numbers in a number sentence. Give a few examples:

$4.8 + \boxed{} = 5$

$2.1 + \boxed{} = 10$

$4.5 + \boxed{} = 9$

---

6. Choosing operations and methods

> **Objective:** Choose and use appropriate number operations and calculation methods to solve problems
> **Leading to:** Using their knowledge to create their own number story problems to reflect given statements
> **Strand:** Solving problems
> **Topic:** Making decisions

Paired activity
Choosing the appropriate number problems to solve word problems.

Examples
Begin by discussing the four basic steps involved in problem solving with the class:

1. Understand the problem
2. Explore the problem
3. Solve the problem
4. Check the solution

Show the children some problems on the OHP and ask them to tell you which operations are needed to solve them, for example:

1. Katie bought four comics, each costing 75p.
   How much will she have left if she started with £4.05?

2. Flowers are put in bunches of ten. Tess has 348 flowers.
   How many bunches can she make and how many flowers will be left over?

3. Rob bought a camera for £95.70 and a CD player for £65.
   How much did he spend?

4. Tom, Mark and Ben shared £9.68 equally. Tom spent half his share on a book.
   How much did he then have?

5. Jane earned £5.50 per hour and worked five hours. She had to spend £3.60 on bus fares.
   How much of her wages was she left with?

Give the pairs of children the problem cards on photocopiable sheet 8 and ask them to work out which operations are required to give a solution and then to solve them:

Plenary
Discuss the problem-solving activities that the children have been working on. Choose some pairs to explain their work.
Tell the children that because they have worked so well, next time they will be making up their own 'number story' problems from statements that you will be giving them. Show some examples of what they will be doing:

Statement: 1435 + 3245 = 4680
Possible problem: Arsenal Football Club sold 1435 tickets for their league match on Tuesday and 3245 on Wednesday.
How many tickets did they sell altogether on those two days?

Statement: 689 – 65 = 624
Possible problem: Tom had collected 689 stamps. He gave his collection of French stamps away. He had 65 French stamps.
How many did he have left?

7. Angles

> **Objective:** Investigate a general statement about angles
> **Leading to:** Investigating angles in shapes
> **Strand:** Solving problems
> **Topic:** Reasoning about numbers and shapes

Group activity
Finding examples that match a general statement.

Give the children a statement to investigate, such as: *Angles on a straight line add up to 180°.*
The children need to use rulers and protractors to draw two angles on a straight line.
Measure them and see if the total size of the angles comes to 180°. They should draw several of these, measuring accurately each time, as proof that the statement is true. They could try with different numbers of angles along the line and see if they get the same result.

Plenary
Discuss the work of the groups. Decide what the investigation has concluded.
Tell the children that during the next session they will be making a further investigation of angles, but those inside shapes.

Example
Find out how many degrees there are inside a triangle. How can this help you to find out how many are in a quadrilateral, pentagon and hexagon?
(There are 180° in a triangle: use this to find those in the other shapes.)

**A quadrilateral is made up from two triangles.
So its degrees equal 360°.**

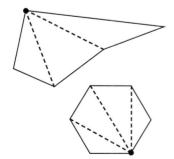

**A pentagon is made up from three triangles.
So its degrees equal 540°.**

**A hexagon is made up from four triangles.
So its degrees equal 720°.**

8. Time

> **Objective:** Read the time to the minute on a 24-hour digital clock
> **Leading to:** Using their knowledge to read timetables using 24-hour digital clock times
> **Strand:** Measures
> **Topic:** Time

Paired activity

Reading the time to the minute on a 24-hour digital clock.

Give the children some digital clock faces with 12-hour and 24-hour times on and ask them to order them from earliest time to latest. Ask them to record the order of times in analogue, 12-hour digital and 24-hour digital:

Plenary

Hold up some of the time cards and ask the children to tell you what time it says in the 'other' types of time.
Tell the children that next time they will be using their knowledge of time to solve problems and read timetables. Give them the example on photocopiable sheet 9, and ask them the following questions:

What time does the 09:40 from Birmingham New Street arrive at Reading?
Which is the fastest train from Birmingham New Street to Reading?
How long does it take the 13:55 from Oxford to reach Reading?
You have to arrive in Oxford at 2:00 p.m. Which train would you catch from Coventry?

Year 6

9. Multiplying and dividing by 10

> **Objective:** Multiply and divide whole numbers and decimals by 10, 100 or 1000
> **Leading to:** Putting this knowledge into a practical context
> **Strand:** Numbers and the number system
> **Topic:** Place value and ordering

Paired activity

Demonstrating an understanding of multiplying and dividing by 10, 100 and 1000.

Begin by asking the children what happens when you multiply a number by 10. Expect answers such as "It gets 10 times bigger"; "The digits move a place to the left". Repeat for 100 and 1000. Ask the children to demonstrate on the board:

Th	H	T	U		10's Th	Th	H	T	U	
			6					4	9	
		6	0	x10			4	9	0	x10
	6	0	0	x100		4	9	0	0	x100
6	0	0	0	x1000	4	9	0	0	0	x1000

Repeat this for division:

Th	H	T	U				10's Th	Th	H	T	U		
		3	6				6	8	3	0	0		
		3 .	6	÷10				6	8	3	0	0	÷10
		0 .	36	÷100					6	8	3	0	÷100
		0 .	036	÷1000						6	8 .	3	÷1000

Ask the children to use their digit cards to generate numbers for their partner to multiply and divide by 10, 100 and 1000, read and record their answers. There are digit cards on photocopiable sheet 1.

Plenary

Ask some children to pick three digit cards. Ask others to x and ÷ by 10, 100 and 1000, explaining as they do exactly what it is that they are doing, i.e. "I am going to make this number 1000 times smaller, so I must move all the digits to the right three times. I am dividing by 10 and then 10 and then 10 again."
Tell the children that, as they have achieved this objective, next time they will be using this knowledge to look at some practical examples in measurement.

Example

Look at a metre stick. Name something that is about the same length. Now name something that is about 10m in length. Build up a table, recognising that it involves multiplying or dividing by 10.

Distance to town centre	10000m
From the school to the park	1000m
Length of the playground fence	100m
Length of the swimming pool	10m
Height of the shelves	1m
Length of a pencil	0.1m
Width of a thumb nail	0.01m
Thickness of a 5p coin	0.001m

Discuss how many centimetres and millimetres make up 0.1m, 0.01m and 0.001m.

10. Number sequences

> **Objective:** Recognise and extend number sequences by finding and continuing a pattern
> **Leading to:** Using their knowledge to work out a triangular number pattern
> **Strand:** Numbers and the number system
> **Topic:** Properties of numbers and number sequences

Paired activity

Investigating patterns in number.

Begin by demonstrating square patterns using cubes on a OHP:

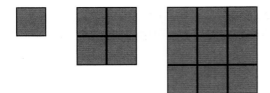

Ask the children how many cubes make each square. Ask them to predict the size of the next one. In pairs ask them to build up a sequence of seven squares in this way. Once they have, ask them to look for a number pattern and then predict the sizes of the next five squares. These are all square numbers and run in the sequence of 1, 4, 9, 16, 25, 36, 49, 64, 81, 100, 121, 144.

Plenary
During the plenary, ask the children what they have discovered. If any have noticed the square number pattern, ask them to prove it.
Tell them that, as a result of their success today, tomorrow they will be investigating another pattern. Write this sequence of numbers on the board: 1, 3, 6, 10, 15, 21... What do they think the next number will be? Tell them that tomorrow they might consider using triangles to help them to investigate the pattern. The pattern is a triangular one and can be shown using triangles in 'dot' form, as shown below:

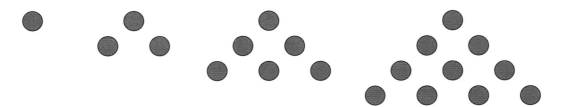

11. Fractions, decimals and percentages

> **Objective:** Understand percentages as the number of parts in every hundred, recognise the equivalence between percentages and fractions and decimals
> **Leading to:** Using their knowledge to solve problems
> **Strand:** Numbers and the number system
> **Topic:** Fractions, decimals and percentages

Paired/small-group activity
Working out equivalences, using a calculator when appropriate.

Begin by using the 'show me strip'. Ask the children to show you various fractions, decimals and percentages by putting a paper clip on the correct part of the strip:

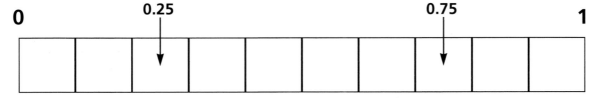

Show me ½, 75%, ⅛, 0.25, ¼, ¾, 10%, ¹/₁₀, 0.1, etc. Ask questions such as: "What do you notice about 10%, 1/10, and 0.1?"
Remind the children how to change fractions to decimals using a calculator.
Give each pair or small group the fraction, decimal and percentage grid on photocopiable sheet 10, and ask them to fill the lines up.

Plenary
Choose some of the children to tell the others what their equivalences were and how they worked them out.
Tell the children that during the next lesson they will be using their ability to solve problems. Tell them that they will need to decide whether working out a fraction or a percentage of an amount of money is more efficient, i.e. working out ¼ may be easier than finding 25%. Give them the example on photocopiable sheet 10. When the children have completed the chart, ask them the following questions:

1. Sarah bought two single CDs and an album in the sale. How much did she spend?
2. Ben had £10. He bought a CD album in the sale. How much change was he given?
3. My mum and dad wanted to buy a DVD player. They had saved £280. How much more did they need to buy one in the sale?
4. What is the difference in price between the CD player before and during the sale?

12. Distributive law of multiplication

> **Objective:** Understand and use when appropriate the principles of the distributive law of multiplication
> **Leading to:** Using when appropriate the associative law of multiplication
> **Strand:** Calculations
> **Topic:** Understanding multiplication

Paired activity
Solving calculations using the distributive law.

Discuss examples of when this method would be used efficiently to solve calculations, using examples such as:

$$46 \times 98 = (46 \times 100) - (46 \times 2)$$
$$= 4600 - 92$$
$$= 4508$$

$$15 \times 47 = (15 \times 50) - (15 \times 3)$$
$$= 750 - 45$$
$$= 705$$

Give the pairs of children calculations to work through (differentiated of course!).

Plenary
During the plenary take feedback on how the children got on and ask their opinions of the value of this method of multiplication. Tell them that during their next lesson they will be thinking about multiplying using a different method (the associative law). Show them an example:

```
3.6 x 40  =  (3.6 x 10) x 2 x 2
          =  36 x 2 x 2
          =  72 x 2
          =  144
```

Give them a few similar examples to do mentally.

13. Written methods for division

Objective: Develop and refine written methods for the division of whole numbers
Leading to: Developing written methods for the division of decimals
Strand: Calculations
Topic: Pencil and paper procedures (division)

Paired activity
Answering division calculations using the written method in as few steps as possible.

Remind the children of grouping. Write an example of a calculation on the board.
Estimate first:
$864 \div 24$
Estimate might be 40 because there are 40 20s in 800.
Take off multiples of 10 first, as far as possible.

```
        864
        240   (10 x 24)
        624
        240   (10 x 24)
        384
        240   (10 x 24)
        144
        120   (5 x 24)
         24
         24   (1 x 24)
```

Answer = 36

Give the groups of children a challenge: "Try to answer the calculations you are to be given in the fewest number of steps possible." Demonstrate first:

$365 \div 12$

Estimate: 36 because $365 \div$ by 10 is just over 36.

```
        365
        360   (30 x 12)
          5
```

Answer = $30 \frac{5}{12}$

Provide the children with a variety of calculations and remind them to put remainders as a fraction.

Plenary

Work through a few of the calculations with the children and see which groups have managed to use the fewest steps possible. Tell the children that during their next lesson they will be dividing decimal numbers in the same way and putting remainders as decimal places instead of fractions. Give an example:

$87.5 \div 7$ Estimate: $80 \div 8 = 10$

```
        87.5
        70.0  (10 x 7)
        17.5
        14.0  (2 x 7)
         3.5
         3.5  (0.5 x 7)
           0
```

Answer = 12.5

14. Reading from scales

> **Objective:** Record readings from scales to a suitable degree of accuracy
> **Leading to:** Converting smaller units into larger ones and vice versa
> **Strand:** Measures
> **Topic:** Length, mass and capacity

Group activity

Estimating and measuring items on a variety of scales with accuracy.

Have your classroom arranged so that the children can work in small groups at tables. They will need to complete tasks at one table during a given time and then move on to the next to complete tasks at that and then on to the final set of tasks at the third table. Six groups would be ideal and two lots of three activities:

Tables 1 and 2: weight. Provide a tub of sand, flour or something similar, eight different sized containers, three sets of calibrated scales, some paper and pens for recording, and activity cards 1 –3 on photocopiable sheet 11.
Tables 3 and 4: capacity. Provide a jug or two of water, eight different sized containers, three measuring jugs, some paper and pens for recording, and activity cards 4-6 on photocopiable sheet 11.
Tables 5 and 6: length. Provide a variety of items: rulers, metre sticks, tape measures, paper and pens for recording, and question cards 7-10 on photocopiable sheet 11.

Plenary

Discuss what the groups have been doing. Ask how accurate their estimating was. Invite some children to demonstrate an activity to the rest of the class.
Tell the children that during their next lesson they will be looking at the measurements they found today and converting them into larger and smaller units. Give a few examples:

The rubber band's width was 2mm. What is this as a centimetre measurement? (0.2cm) As a metre measurement? (0.002m)

The capacity of the smallest container was 75ml. What is this as a litre measurement? (0.075l)

The weight of the sand in the largest container was 2½kg. What is this as a gram measurement? (2500g)

15. Areas

> **Objective:** Measure and calculate the area of compound shapes using the formula for finding the area of a rectangle
> **Leading to:** Using their knowledge of area to find lengths, breadths and heights of boxes and also surface areas of boxes
> **Strand:** Measures
> **Topic:** Area and perimeter

Paired activity
Calculating the areas of compound shapes.

Begin by asking the children to find areas of a few rectangles:

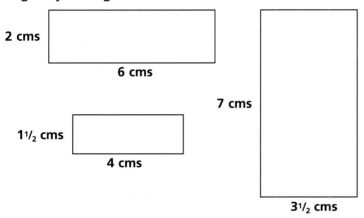

Ask the children to think of a formula that will always work, i.e. length x breadth. Discuss how this can be useful if they need to work out the areas of other compound shapes. Demonstrate using examples such as:

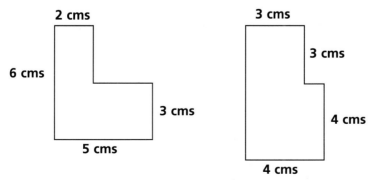

Give the children some shapes as above and ask them to calculate their areas.

Plenary
Work through a few examples of the children's calculations, asking them to demonstrate how they made them.

Tell the children that, because they are so good at doing this, next time they will be working out the surface areas of boxes and also calculating lengths and breadths of boxes. Give the children at least one example of both.
Use a real box and measure the length and breadth of the necessary sides.

Example

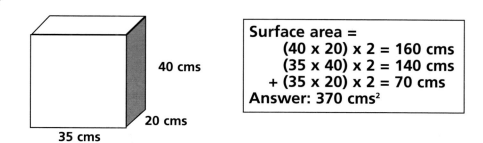

Surface area =
     (40 x 20) x 2 = 160 cms
     (35 x 40) x 2 = 140 cms
   + (35 x 20) x 2 = 70 cms
Answer: 370 cms²

Draw a box shape on the board and write areas inside the three visible sections.
The children need to try to work out the length, breadth and height from the areas.

Example

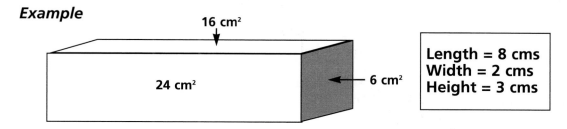

Length = 8 cms
Width = 2 cms
Height = 3 cms

16. Using co-ordinates

Objective: Read and plot points using co-ordinates beyond the first quadrant
Leading to: Reflecting polygons from one quadrant into the others
Strand: Shape and space
Topic: Position and direction

Paired activity
Drawing shapes by plotting and labelling the vertices in the four quadrants.

Begin by reminding the children of the work they did in Year 5, using co-ordinates in the first quadrant. These demonstrations are best carried out using acetates and an OHP.

Example

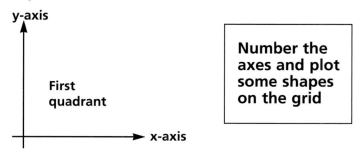

Number the axes and plot some shapes on the grid

Now introduce the 'four quadrant grid':

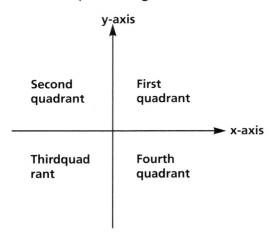

Plot the numbers from –6 to 6 on both axes. Ask the children to mark certain points that you give them in the correct place. Draw three vertices of a square in three of the quadrants and ask the children to work out where the fourth would come.

Give the pairs of children activity cards similar to the ones below to complete on co-ordinates that they draw themselves:

Draw a pentagon. Write down the co-ordinates of the verticles. Do the same for a hexagon and a heptagon.	**Plot these points: (-1,1), (2,5) and (6,2) To make a square where will you plot the forth vertex?**	**Draw a dodecagon that has three of its vertices in each quadrant. Write down the co-ordinates of each vertex.**

Plenary

Invite some of the pairs to demonstrate their work, explaining clearly what they have done.

Tell the children that now they can plot co-ordinates in four quadrants, during the next lesson they will be reflecting polygons drawn in one quadrant into one or two of the other three. Demonstrate an example, asking the children what the co-ordinates of the vertices will be.

Example

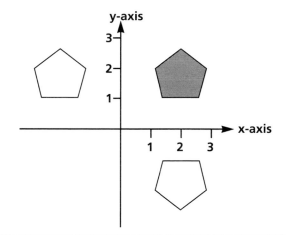

Photocopiable Sheet 7
The Thermometer Game

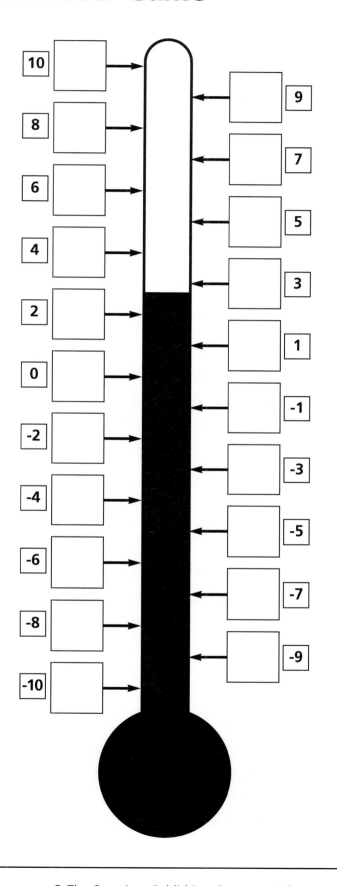

Photocopiable Sheet 8
Choosing operations and methods

John has £2.80. His sister Ruth, who is three years older than John, had £3.41 more than he did. How much did Ruth have?

Barry worked for 18 hours at £3.50 per hour. He was given a bonus for good work. How much did he receive in total?

Jim left home at half past 10. He walked for 45 minutes. Then he stopped to have a drink and something to eat. At what time did he stop?

Alan and Bill both ran 10km. They both got very hot and tired. Alan started a half past 3 and finished at 4 o'clock. Bill took 35 minutes. Who was faster?

Mary has £20. She would like to buy some shoes costing £15, a bag costing £23 and a pair of jeans costing £25. How much more does she need?

Photocopiable Sheet 9

Time

Birmingham New Street	09:40	10:05	11:05	12:35
Birmingham International	09:50	10:15	11:15	12:45
Coventry	10:10	10:30	11:30	13:00
Leamington Spa	10:25		11:45	13:15
Banbury	10:45		12:05	
Oxford	11:05	11:20	12:25	13:55
Reading	11:30	11:55	12:50	14:25

Photocopiable Sheet 10
Fractions, decimals and percentages

Fraction	Decimal	Percentage
1/2		
	0.6	
	0.15	
		75%
		5%
4/5		
5/8		

Rixons the music shop in town had a sale. Complete this chart to show by how much their prices were reduced and what the new prices are.

Item	Price	Reduction	Sale Price
CD Player	£125	20%	
CDs (singles)	£3.50	1/2 price	
CDs (albums)	£12.90	1/3 off	
DVD Player	£460	25%	
DVDs	£18.60	5%	
Personal Stereo	£25	10%	

Photocopiable Sheet 11
Length, mass and capacity

1

Fill the smallest container with sand.
Pour the sand into the scales.
What is its weight?
How much more sand do you need to make it weigh the same as the next container?

2

Fill the largest container with sand.
Pour the sand into the scales.
What is its weight?
What is the difference in weight between this and the lightest?

3

Fill all the containers with sand.
Estimate their weights and order from lightest to heaviest.
Weigh each one in turn, find out how accurate your estimates and your ordering were.

4

Fill the smallest container with water.
Pour the water into the measuring jug.
What is its capacity?
How much more water do you need to make it fill the next container?

5

Fill the largest container with water.
Pour the water into the measuring jug.
What is its capacity?
What is the difference in capacity between this and and that of the smallest container?

6

Fill all the containers with water.
Estimate their capacity and order from least to greatest.
Measure each one in turn, find out how accurate your estimates and your ordering were.

7

What is the width of the one pence coin?
From this work out the width of a 'tower' of 12 one pence coins.

8

What is the width of the rubber band?
Can you find one that is wider?
Can you find one that is narrower?

9

What is the perimeter of the classroom?
If the perimeter was twice as big, draw five possible plans of how it could look.

Chapter 3
Links to other maths topics and curriculum areas

The Framework for Teaching Mathematics has a very helpful section on making links between the subjects. It states that 'you need to look for opportunities for drawing mathematical experience out of a wide range of children's activities.'
Maths contributes to many subjects in the primary curriculum, often in practical ways, and these links often help to validate the purposes of maths.
Maths and other areas of curriculum subjects can complement each other. It is important that links are made as it helps the children to see the relevance of what they are learning in the overall picture of their education. It is often too easy to treat the curriculum subjects as isolated areas that must be covered. Linking makes it all the more real to the children as it can put what they are learning into contexts they can appreciate.

Subject links (extracts from the NNS Framework):

English: Maths lessons can help develop and support pupils' literacy skills by teaching mathematical vocabulary and technical terms, asking children to read and interpret problems to identify the mathematical content, and by encouraging them to explain, argue and present conclusions to others.
Science: Almost every scientific investigation or experiment is likely to require one or more of the mathematical skills of classifying, counting, measuring, calculating, estimating and recording in tables and graphs.
Art, D & T: Measurements are often needed in art and design and technology. Many patterns and constructions are based on spatial ideas and properties of shapes including symmetry.
ICT: Children will apply and use mathematics in a variety of ways when they solve problems using ICT. For example, they will collect and classify data, enter it into data-handling software, produce graphs and tables, and interpret and explain their results.
History, geography and RE: In various circumstances children will collect data by counting and measuring, use co-ordinates, ideas of angle, direction, position, scale and ratio. Patterns of days of the week, the calendar, annual festivals and passages of time all have a mathematical basis.
PE and music: These often require measurement of height, distance and time, counting, symmetry, movement, position and direction.

Plenary sessions can be used to discuss work carried out in the objectives taught and linked to work that has been or will be studied in subjects such those mentioned.

This chapter is designed to show where some of the possible links are, in order to get you thinking about making links in literacy, science, history, geography, art and PE, as well as other maths topics.

Literacy

Links between numeracy and literacy are plentiful.

In the Curriculum Guidelines for English, it states that children should be taught to:

- ✪ Speak clearly, fluently and confidently to different people;
- ✪ Listen, understand and respond to others;
- ✪ Join as members of a group;
- ✪ Participate in a range of drama activities;
- ✪ Be part of group discussion and interaction;
- ✪ Be taught grammatical constructions that are characteristic of spoken standard English and how language varies

In maths all of these are encouraged as a matter of course by, for example:

- ✪ Explaining strategies to others;
- ✪ Listening to and discussing other children's methods of working out calculations;
- ✪ Working on activities in a group;
- ✪ Imagining and acting out problems in the problem-solving strand;
- ✪ Discussing and interacting with each other in group work;
- ✪ Learning, understanding and using new vocabulary.

Year 5

1. Mental addition

> **Objective:** Add mentally two numbers, within a range of 100 to about 500, by partitioning into hundreds, tens and ones
> **Strand:** Calculations
> **Topic:** Mental calculation strategies (+ and -)

Possible activities
Give pairs of children a selection of about 15 cards with a number between 100 and 500 written on each. Ask them to place the cards in a pile face down in front of them.
Give them a time limit and ask them to pick two cards and total them. How many sets of two cards can they total in the time allowed?
Call out pairs of numbers, ask the children to add them mentally and write down their answer on a piece of paper.
Write some pairs of numbers on the board. Give the children a minute to total them and show their answer using digit cards.

Plenary
During the plenary, display a coding card with letters of the alphabet and numbers, e.g. A = 50, B = 100, C = 150, D = 200, E = 250, F = 350, etc. See photocopiable sheet 12. Write on the board some words that have common letter strings but different pronunciations, e.g. rough, cough, bough. Discuss the words with the children. Ask the children to find the value of these words, i.e. rough = 900 + 750 + 1050 + 350 + 400 = 3450.

Ask – "Is there a quick way to find the total of these particular words?" Someone should be able to tell you that if you work out the value of the 'ough', then you just need to add on the other letters each time.

Then tell the children that during their next literacy lesson, they will be working with words similar to the ones that they have used during this plenary session and totalling their values.

2. 2-D shape vocabulary

Objective: Use, read and write, spelling correctly, the vocabulary from the previous year and extend
Strand: Shape and space
Topic: Properties of 2-D shapes

Possible activities

Discuss the vocabulary of the following descriptions of shapes: flat, curved, straight, round, corner, pointed, face, side, edge, centre, radius, diameter, angle, congruent, regular, irregular, concave, convex. What does each one mean? Can children think of a shape that shows any of these descriptions?

Ask the children in pairs to pick some shapes and describe them to each other using as many of the vocabulary words as they can which are appropriate. Then they should record their descriptions by drawing the shape and making labels for it.

Ask the children to pick three shapes and put them together to make another shape. Make a template on card of the new shape and then make a pattern or picture that shows the shape repeated in different positions to show congruency.

Plenary

During the plenary revise the vocabulary of the lesson. Ask some children to show their pictures of congruent shapes. Have prepared the vocabulary on pieces of card and ask other children to select the words that are appropriate to the congruent shapes and 'Blu-Tack' them to the board.

Tell the children that this work will be used in their next literacy lesson when they will be making up a glossary or word bank for these words.

3. Fractions and percentages

Objective: Understand percentage as the number of parts in every hundred
Strand: Numbers and the number system
Topic: Fractions, decimals and percentages

Possible activities

Give groups of children some newspapers (advertising ones would be best) and ask them to find all the references to percentages. Record their findings. Discuss what they think is meant by them.

Ask the children to collect 100 multilink cubes and identify what percentage of them are which colour.

Plenary
Ask the children to feed back to the rest of the class, the work that they have been doing. Ask them what they now know about percentages. Tell the children that during their next literacy lesson they will be using what they have learnt today to help them write instructions about 'how to find a percentage.'

4. Solving story problems

Objective: Solve 'story' problems about numbers in real life, choosing the appropriate operation and method of calculation
Strand: Solving problems
Topic: 'Real life' problems

Possible activity
Ask the children to work in groups of three or four. Give them a 'story' problem. They need to read it through carefully and then answer the questions, thinking about the following:

- ✪ What is the question asking us to find out?
- ✪ What information in the story is relevant?
- ✪ How are we going to solve the question?
- ✪ What would be a sensible estimate?
- ✪ Does our answer seem sensible and is it close to our estimate?

There is a story problem on photocopiable sheet 13.

Plenary
Work through the whole problem with the class, asking various children how they worked out their answers and what information they needed to use to help them.
Tell the children that during their next literacy lesson, they will be writing their own number 'story' problem to bring back to the next numeracy lesson for their friends to answer.

Year 6

5. Imperial and metric units

> **Objective:** Know the approximate equivalence between commonly used imperial units and metric units
> **Strand:** Measures
> **Topic:** Length, mass and capacity

Possible activity

Collect some measuring equipment that has both metric and imperial measurements. Ask the children in groups to:

- ✪ Measure water into a jug and work out how many pints are the same as a litre.
- ✪ Weigh 1kg of sand and find out how much that is in pounds.
- ✪ Use a tape measure to find out how many feet there are in a metre and from this knowledge, work out how many feet there are in a km.
- ✪ Use their knowledge of how many feet there are in a metre (and a calculator) and the information that there are 12 inches in a foot to work out how many centimetres there are in an inch.
- ✪ Tell them how many feet there are in a mile and ask them to calculate how many kilometres there are in one mile.

Plenary

Discuss with the class all the equivalences that they found and display them on the board. How accurate were they? Have the actual conversions handy so that you can show them. Tell the children that during their next literacy lesson they will be making up short rhymes to help them remember these equivalences, for example:

> *'Two and a quarter pounds of jam*
> *Is round about one kilogram.'*

6. More story problems

> **Objective:** Solve 'story' problems about numbers in real life, choosing the appropriate operation and method of calculation
> **Strand:** Solving problems
> **Topic:** 'Real life' problems

Possible activity

Ask the children to work in groups of three or four. Give them a 'story' problem. They need to read it through carefully and then answer the questions, thinking about the following:

- ✪ What is the question asking us to find out?
- ✪ What information in the story is relevant?
- ✪ How are we going to solve the question?
- ✪ What would be a sensible estimate?
- ✪ Does our answer seem sensible and is it close to our estimate?

There is a story problem on photocopiable sheet 14.

Extension activity
Draw a line graph to show the times and events of the day, beginning with leaving home and finishing with the family arriving back at their house.

Plenary
Work through the first part of the whole problem with the class, asking various children how they worked out their answers and what information they needed to use to help them. Tell the children that during their next literacy lesson, they will be writing their own number 'story' problem to bring back to the next numeracy lesson for their friends to answer.

7. Handling data

> **Objective:** Solve a problem by collecting, organising, representing, extracting and interpreting data in graphs
> **Strand:** Handling data
> **Topic:** Organising and interpreting data

Possible activity
A data-handling activity in which these five aspects need to be considered:

- ✪ Specifying the problem
- ✪ Planning
- ✪ Collecting data
- ✪ Processing and representing
- ✪ Interpreting and discussion

For details of these aspects see links with Science p.50.

The problem could be: Where shall we go for our summer holiday?
During the planning stage the children need to decide what type of holiday they would like to go on, which countries they would like to consider and what the weather should be like.
In pairs or small groups, children need to collect information from holiday brochures or the Internet, selecting a few to choose from.
Display on a graph the relevant information, which will help them come to a conclusion as to which holiday they would choose.

Plenary
As a class discuss what the children have been doing and what their graphs show. Tell the children that during their next literacy lesson they will be using their graphs to write a journalistic type account of where to go and where not to go this summer.

8. Probability

> **Objective:** Use the language associated with probability to discuss events, including those with equally likely outcomes
> **Strand:** Handling Data
> **Topic:** Probability

Possible activities

Discuss events which might have two equally likely outcomes, e.g. a new baby is equally likely to be a boy or a girl; if I roll a dice I am just as likely to roll an even number as an odd number.

Think about a 1 – 6 dice and place the probability of the following statements on a scale from impossible to certain:

 a. rolling a 4
 b. rolling an even number
 c. rolling a number greater than 2
 d. rolling zero
 e. rolling a number between 0 and 7

Work in pairs to record the outcomes of tossing a coin: make 20 tosses and record the results. Think about questions such as:: 'Did heads and tails each come up 10 times?'

Plenary

Discuss probability statements from real life, e.g. when I am older I will get married; when I am 18 I will go to university; I will win the lottery; I will grow taller than my father. Tell the children that during their next literacy lesson they will be writing about what their future has in store for them. They will be thinking about what they would like to do and then thinking about the probability of it actually happening.

Science

Links between numeracy and science are plentiful. They mostly come under the strand of Handling data, although working with numbers and measures obviously plays an important part.

In the Curriculum Guidelines for Science, it states that children should be taught to:

- ✪ Ask questions that can be investigated scientifically and decide how they might find answers to them;
- ✪ Think about what might happen or try things out before deciding what to do;
- ✪ Check observations and measurements by repeating them where appropriate;
- ✪ Use a wide range of methods, including diagrams, drawings, tables, bar charts, line graphs and ICT, to communicate data in an appropriate and systematic manner;.
- ✪ Make comparisons and identify simple patterns or associations in their own observations and measurements or other data;
- ✪ Review their work and the work of others and describe its significance and limitations.

In maths all of these are encouraged in different ways, for example:

- ✪ Asking questions such as: "Which is the best way to answer this calculation?", "What would happen if I did it this way?"; "What do I need to know to solve this problem?"
- ✪ Estimating answers;
- ✪ Recording measurements with length, mass, capacity and time;
- ✪ Solving a problem by collecting, representing and interpreting data;
- ✪ Making comparisons and identifying patterns in number, shapes and measures;
- ✪ Checking and explaining strategies, deciding on the efficiency of their methods.

The Handling data strand is probably the best way to link the two subjects.
There are five aspects of data handling in numeracy that need to be considered:

- ✪ Specifying the problem – formulating questions in terms of the data that is needed and the type of inferences that can be made from them.
- ✪ Planning – deciding what data needs collecting, including sample size and data format and what statistical analysis needs to be carried out.
- ✪ Collecting data – from a variety of appropriate sources including experiments, surveys and primary and secondary data.
- ✪ Processing and representing – including lists, tables and charts.
- ✪ Interpreting and discussion – relating the summarised data to the initial question.

It is often appropriate to use a problem that needs solving in science to satisfy these requirements. The interpreting and discussion aspect can be achieved during the plenary session and then taken into the science lesson to use as needed.
This part of the chapter concentrates on possible problems that can be solved in numeracy and then taken into the science lesson.

Year 5

1. Keeping healthy

> **Objectives**
> How to measure their pulse rate and relate it to heart beat
> To repeat measurements of pulse rate
> To represent data about resting pulse rate in a bar chart and to say what this shows

Possible science activities

(a) Ask the children about the relationship between heartbeat and pulse. Explain to the children that pulse rate is measured as beats per unit time (minute).

(b) Show the children how to measure resting pulse rate and ask them to take and record their own several times.

(c) Ask the children to suggest why they did not get the same result each time and why it is important to make several measurements.

(d) Ask them to contribute the result they think is the most accurate to a class record of resting pulse rate.

(e) Help the children to convert this into a bar chart where data is grouped.

(f) Ask the children questions about the bar chart, e.g.
- ✪ Which was the most common range for pulse rate?
- ✪ What were the highest and lowest pulse rates?
- ✪ Were these very common?

Numeracy: Data handling lesson

Remind the children of the unit that is being studied in their science lessons.
Explain that today they will be finding out something that will help them in science.
Follow the science activity parts a, b, c, d and e above.

Plenary

Discuss the findings displayed from the bar charts and ask questions similar to the ones in part (f) above.
Take this conclusion back into the next science lesson, when children will be speculating about factors which could change the pulse rate and investigating the relationship between exercise and pulse rate. This could lead into another numeracy lesson where the children can construct continuous data graphs.

2. Earth, Sun and Moon

> **Objectives**
> To know that the sun rises in the general direction of the East and sets in the general direction of the West
> To make observations of where the sun rises and sets and to recognise the patterns in these
> To present times of sunrise and sunset in a graph and to recognise trends and patterns in the data

Possible science activities

(a) Ask the children to use a compass to observe and record, on several days in the winter, the direction of the Sun or of the shadows from the Sun when it has just risen and just before it sets.

(b) Provide secondary data about times of sunrise and sunset and help them to present this data as a graph and to identify patterns in the data.

(c) Discuss with the children whether it is dark or light when they get up in the winter and summer and what sorts of activities they can do on winter and summer evenings.

Numeracy: Handling data lesson

Remind the class of the work they are doing in science.

Using secondary data from ICT sources or the newspaper, follow through part (b) of the science activity above. Their graph needs to be a line graph as this is continuous data.

Plenary

Invite some of the children to explain their graphs to the rest of the class.

Discuss part (c) of the science activity above.

Tell the children that they will be using this information in their next science lesson when they will be considering the Earth's orbit around the Sun during a year and how our seasons come about.

Year 6

3. How we see things

Objectives:
To identify factors which might affect the size and position of the shadow of an object
To investigate how changing one factor causes a shadow to change
To consider trends in results and to decide whether there are results which do not fit the pattern
To check measurements by repeating them

Possible science activities

(a) Remind the children of shadow formation using an opaque object, e.g. a cardboard figure.

(b) Ask them to explore ways in which the shadow of the figure can be made to change.

(c) Ask the children to suggest questions they could investigate, e.g. What happens to the size of the shadow when you move the figure nearer to the light?

(d) Help the children to decide how to carry out the investigation, including deciding on the measurements they are going to take.

(e) Ask the children to record results and help them to present them in a line graph.

(f) Talk with the children about patterns in the results and, if necessary, encourage them to repeat measurements to check them.

Numeracy: Handling data lesson

Remind the children of what they are studying in science. Tell them that to help their shadow investigation –'What happens to the size of the shadow when you move the figure nearer to the light?' – they are going to carry out the measuring and representing of their findings during this numeracy lesson.

In groups, ask the children to make eight measurements beginning with the size of the figure furthest away from the light and, gradually moving it closer to the light, make seven more measurements.

Ask them to make a line graph to show these measurements. The horizontal axis could be distance from light and the vertical the size of figure in centimetres.

Plenary

Look at all the graphs. Do they show any similarities? Discuss findings.

Can the children come up with a conclusion to take back to their next science lesson?

4. Forces in action

> **Objectives**
>
> To know how much an elastic band stretches depends on the force acting on it
>
> To make careful measurements of length
>
> To represent data in a line graph and use this to identify patterns in the data

Possible science activities

(a) Ask the children to explore what happens to the length of an elastic band when weights are suspended from it. Suggest they make measurements so that they can look for a pattern in their data.

(b) Help children to represent data collected as a line graph.

(c) Talk about the patterns in the graphs and ask children to make predictions from the graph, e.g. the length of the elastic band when another weight is added.

(d) Help the children test their predictions, ensuring they do not over-stretch the band.

Numeracy: Handling data lesson

Explain to the children that during their numeracy lesson today, they will be doing some work related to their science topic of Forces in action.

Using weights form 50g to 200g follow through part (a) and (b) of the science activity outlined above. Their graph will be for continuous data, so the axes will need to be labelled with the weights used and the length of stretch in centimetres and started with the lightest weight moving to the heaviest.

Plenary

During the plenary, ask the children to discuss their findings as represented by their line graphs. Then follow part (d) above, making predictions of what will happen if they use various weights less than 50g and more than 200g.

Tell the children that in their next science lesson, they will be testing their predictions.

History

Links between numeracy and history are evident in the strands of Calculations and Solving problems.

In the Curriculum Guidelines for History, it states that children should be taught to:

- ✪ Place events, people and changes into correct periods of time;
- ✪ Use dates and vocabulary relating to the passing of time.

In maths, this Attainment Target can be supported during the teaching of different topics, for example:

- ✪ Number operations and the relationship between them;
- ✪ Developing rapid recall of number facts;
- ✪ Developing a range of mental strategies for finding, from known facts, those that they cannot recall;
- ✪ Carrying out simple calculations;
- ✪ Choose sensible calculation methods to solve whole-number problems.

Years 5 and 6

For both of the following units use a similar number line activity and plenary as shown below.

1. Unit 13: How has life in Britain changed since 1948?

What are the changes in work, home life, popular culture, population and technology in Britain since 1948? When did these changes happen?

> **Objective**
> To know what changes have occurred to the way of life of people since 1948

Possible activities
Talk about what it means to do an enquiry. Introduce the two main questions and explain that there are five topics to research in groups:
(a) Work
(b) Home life
(c) Popular culture
(d) Population
(e) Technology

During history sessions allow the children to make an in-depth study of their topic. When this is complete, they should take their findings to their next numeracy lesson.

Possible numeracy activity
As part of a session on ordering numbers, for the group part of the lesson use the information gleaned during history to enable the children to present their findings on a time line.

Plenary
As a class discuss each group's findings using their time lines. Tell the children that during their next history lesson, they will be considering the most important changes found in their particular topic and how they have affected life today, and place them on a class time line.

2. Unit 19: What were the effects of Tudor exploration?

Why did the Tudors explore outside Europe?

Objectives
To locate the Tudor period in relation to other periods of British history
To find out the reasons for Tudor exploration

Possible activities
Use a time line to establish the chronological periods between the present and the Tudor period.
Discuss and list reasons why people explore the world and space today.
Establish with the children that the Tudors wanted to explore because they were:

(a) Looking for new countries in which to trade wool and other goods and bring back expensive items, e.g. spices and furs, to sell at home
(b) Looking for a place where they could practise their religion in freedom
(c) Looking for new lands in which to settle

Make a list of these on a flip chart or board.
Ask the children to write paragraphs to show reasons for exploration in Tudor times and today.

Possible numeracy activity
During a lesson on handling data, focus on Venn Diagrams to display information. Practise some examples to do with shape and number. Then ask the children to use the paragraphs they wrote about during history to make a Venn Diagram to display their information clearly. They will need to make one circle represent the Tudor period and the second the present. Where they overlap, this should show the common reasons.

Plenary
During the plenary session, look at the children's Venn Diagrams and discuss what they show. Tell them that during their next history lesson they will be using this information to discuss the reasons that are the same and the ones that are different and why this might be.

Geography

Links between numeracy and geography are obvious when looking at the strand Shape and space within the topics of Position and direction and Movement and angle. Various aspects can be incorporated into Handling data.

In the Curriculum Guidelines for Geography, it states that children should be taught to:

- ✪ Collect and record evidence, e.g. by carrying out a survey of shop functions and showing them on a graph;
- ✪ Communicate in ways appropriate to the task and audience ;
- ✪ Use appropriate geographical vocabulary, e.g. temperature, transport industry;
- ✪ Use atlases and globes, maps and plans at a range of scales, e.g. using contents, keys and grids;
- ✪ Draw maps and plans at a range of scales, e.g. a sketch map of a locality.

In maths all of these are encouraged in different ways, for example:

- ✪ Solve a relevant problem by collecting, organising, representing, extracting and interpreting data in tables, graphs and charts;
- ✪ Use the correct language, symbols and vocabulary associated with number and data;
- ✪ Communicate in spoken, pictorial and written form, using mathematical language and symbols;
- ✪ Present results in an organised way;
- ✪ Recognise positions and directions, and use co-ordinates;
- ✪ Use the eight compass directions N, S, E, W, NE, NW, SE, SW.

Year 5

1. Unit 12:   Should the High Street be closed to traffic?

Objectives
To undertake fieldwork
To collect and record evidence about local traffic issues

Possible geography idea
How big an issue is traffic?
Visit the local high street and ask the children to look at, and collect data about traffic issues, e.g. volume of traffic, parking problems, varying needs of different high street users like shopkeepers, children, senior citizens, businesses.
With the children's help, collate the data they have collected and ask them to record the data on a data file and produce graphs to represent the data. These graphs could be produced using graphing software

Possible numeracy lesson idea
Remind the children about the work that they are doing in geography about the high street. Tell them that today they will be creating their own bar charts or line graphs to represent the data that you put on a computer database from their previous geography lesson. Allow them to decide for themselves which type of graph they think is most suitable.

Plenary
Look at the children's graphs and compare them with the database. Discuss the merits and disadvantages of both forms of representation.
Tell them that during their next geography session, they will interpreting the information with a view to answering the question 'Should the high street be closed to traffic?' and coming up with reasons for their answers.

Year 6

2. Unit 25: Geography and numbers

Objectives
To apply mathematics to work in geography
To use geographical vocabulary
To develop fieldwork skills
To use maps and plans
To investigate the locality of their school

Possible geography idea
There are several suggestions for geography ideas in this unit, involving Problem solving, Measures, Shape and space, and Handling data. For the purposes of this book, the focus idea will be within Shape and space.
Ask the children to build models of ideal settlements using 3-D shapes, recording the range of shapes used and their properties. Children could investigate what the shapes look like from above

Possible numeracy lesson idea
Take the geography idea and use it during a numeracy lesson on properties of 3-D shapes. The children need to sketch the 3-D shapes used and then draw them as 2-D shapes, as if looking at them from above.

Plenary
Show a selection of the children's drawings to the class and ask them which properties link the 3-D and comparable 2-D shapes, i.e. a cylinder would compare with a circle because a cylinder is made with two circular faces.
Tell the children that during their next geography lesson, they will be using their models and sketches to construct plans of their settlements.

Art

Links between numeracy and art are evident in the strand of Shape and space.

In the Curriculum Guidelines for Art, it states that children should be taught about:

- ✪ Visual and tactile elements, including colour, pattern and texture, line and tone, shape, form and space and how these elements can be combined and organised for different purposes;
- ✪ Working on their own, and collaborating with others, on projects in two and three dimensions and on different scales.

In maths, these Attainment Targets can be supported during the teaching of different topics, for example:

- ✪ Describing properties of shapes that they can see or visualise using the related vocabulary;

- ✪ Creating 2-D shapes and 3-D shapes;
- ✪ Recognise reflective symmetry, rotations and translations in familiar 2-D shapes and patterns;
- ✪ Recognise ratio and proportion in paintings.

Years 5 and 6

1. Unit 5C : Talking textiles

Objective:
To investigate and combine visual and tactile qualities of materials and processes and to match these qualities to the purpose of the work

Possible art and design activities

Ask the class to design and make a piece of work that tells a story.
Ask them to experiment with techniques, which should include colouring fabric, layering fabric, applying other materials.
Ask the children to think about:

- ✪ The relative size and proportions of the components of the story, e.g. characters, animals, plants, trees;
- ✪ How each component might be represented;
- ✪ How they use colour, texture, pattern and the sound of materials to communicate the story.

Possible numeracy activity
During a series of lessons on ratio and proportion, show a picture of a child, preferably a photograph. Ask the children what is the difference between the picture and a real child. Expect all kinds of answers, accept them but lead towards the size aspect. Explain that the child is in proportion but smaller and what has been done to make them smaller.
Choose some children to help you. Tell the class that you want to make a drawing of each child, to show how tall they are, but you only have a piece of A3 paper. Ask for suggestions of how to do this. Hopefully someone may suggest something similar to this: for every 10cms tall that they are, draw 1cm. If no-one does, make that suggestion yourself. Measure your helpers, write their heights on the board and convert them to a ratio of 1cm for every 10cms, so if one of your helpers is 1m 45cms tall, their representation on paper will be 14.5cms.
Ask the children to work in pairs to repeat the modelled activity. Then extend this to reducing the height of a table and chair to the same proportion. Ask them to draw their partner standing beside the table and chair.

Plenary
Ask some of the children to show their drawings, explaining how they made them.
Tell the children that they will be using their skills from this numeracy lesson in their next art and design session when they will be adding characters, animals, trees and plants to their picture ensuring that they are in proportion to each other.

PE

Links between numeracy and PE are evident in the strand of Shape and space, topics Position and direction and Movement and angle.

In the Curriculum Guidelines for PE, it states that children should be taught to:

- ✪ Create and perform dances using a range of movement patterns, including those from different times, places and cultures;
- ✪ Respond to a range of stimuli and accompaniment;
- ✪ Create and perform fluent sequences on the floor and using apparatus;
- ✪ nclude variations in level, speed and direction in their sequences.

In the Framework for teaching Mathematics, it is suggested that work covered in the following parts of the numeracy lesson can be reinforced during PE:

- ✪ Follow and give instructions to move in particular directions: face west, turn clockwise through one right angle;
- ✪ Know that after turning through half a turn, or two quarter turns in the same direction you will be facing the opposite direction.

These Year 3 objectives can be extended to Year 5 and 6 objectives and reinforced in dance and gymnastics. Rotations, reflections and translations can also be reinforced during PE.

During plenary sessions make reference to the fact that you will be following up certain activities physically in PE.

Other areas of maths

During plenary sessions for work on numbers and the number system make links to measures and money.

Examples
Ask questions relating the number objectives to money:
The CD player cost £125; in the sale it was reduced by 5%. How much did it cost in the sale?

Ask questions relating to length:
My mum and brother went scuba diving. Mum dived down to 30m; my brother dived to $\frac{1}{4}$ of that depth. How far down did my brother dive?

Ask questions relating to time:
Sam spent 49 minutes doing her homework, 69 minutes watching TV, 54 minutes reading a book and 38 minutes having a bath. How many hours did she spend doing these activities altogether?

Ask questions relating to perimeter:
If each side of a heptagon measures 8cms, what is its perimeter?
What would the perimeter of 2 measure? How about 15?

Photocopiable Sheet 12
Coding Card

A	B	C	D	E	F	G	H	I	J
1	2	3	4	5	6	7	8	9	10

K	L	M	N	O	P	Q	R	S	T
11	12	13	14	15	16	17	18	19	20

U	V	W	X	Y	Z
21	22	23	24	25	26

Photocopiable Sheet 13
The Bank Raid

Sid, Fred, Lucy and Polly are planning a bank raid.

"Here's the timetable," said Sid. "Fred and Lucy will drive to the bank and arrive there at 10:00. It should take you 25 minutes to get there. I will arrive at the bank at 10:20. Polly you must get to the bank 10 minutes before I do and park outside in the getaway car. The hold-up will take place at 25 minutes to 11 and we will leave the bank four minutes after that. We then drive to our hide-out in Soho. It should take 18 minutes to get there.
We are aiming to take £10 000 from the bank. I shall have 2/5 of the money because I organised the job; you three must split the rest of the money up equally between you."

Fill in the missing answers

Fred and Lucy started their drive to the bank at ☐

Polly arrived at the bank at ☐

The hold-up took place ☐ minutes after Sid arrived and ☐ after Polly arrived.

The raid finished at ☐

The traffic was bad and they were ten minutes late getting to their hide-out; they arrived at ☐

Sid collected ☐ from the job.

The others each collected ☐

Unfortunately, the police caught them just after they had shared out the money. This was 1 hour 25 minutes after arriving at their hideout.
The time was ☐

They were arrested five minutes later at ☐

Photocopiable Sheet 14
The Smith Family Outing

The Smith family (mum, dad, Sarah and Sam) went on an outing to Chessington World of Adventures. They left home at 9.00 a.m. one fine Saturday morning. After a 45-minute journey they parked their car and joined the queue to get inside the theme park. They bought a family ticket, which cost the same as two adult tickets at £15.75 each and one child ticket at £12.45. They spent 1 hour 20 minutes waiting in the queue. The first thing that they did when they entered the park was to buy some drinks. They cost £1.15 each. Then they went on a few rides, the best one was Nemesis, which lasted for 13 minutes. They went on that at 12.56. Five minutes later they had their picnic lunch. Mrs Smith had made enough sandwiches so that each of them could have three; she brought enough cakes for one and a half each and four oranges cut into enough segments so that they could have seven each. After lunch they went to look at some of the animals. They saw three lions, four tigers, 12 chimps and six llamas. They saw some penguins and some seals. here were twice as many seals as there were tigers and five times as many penguins as there were seals.
At 5.00 p.m. they left the park. It took them twice as long to get home as it did to get there.
Everyone arrived at home tired and happy after a great day at Chessington World of Adventure.

Read the account of the Smith family outing carefully.
Answer the following questions:

1. When did the Smith family arrive in the car park at Chessington World of Adventure?
2. How much did it cost them to get in?
3. At what time did they enter the theme park itself?
4. How much did they spend on drinks?
5. What time was it when they had their lunch?
6. How many sandwiches did Mrs Smith make?
7. How many cakes did she bring?
8. How many pieces of orange did she cut?
9. How many four-legged animals did they see?
10. What was the total number of seals and penguins that they saw?
11. What time did they get home?
12. How long had they been out of the house that day?

Chapter 4
Problem solving and games

Using and applying the skills that the children have been taught is one of the most important elements of numeracy. Ideas need to be put into context for the children so they can see the sense and relevance of what they have learnt. Many children have difficulty with problem-solving activities; so it is vital to provide them with lots of short sessions in which to practise these skills. The plenary part of the lesson can help, as it is an opportunity to put what they have been learning into a 'real life' situation.

After lessons from the strands of Numbers and the number system, Calculations, Addition, subtraction and mental calculation strategies, incorporate some of the ideas below into your plenaries to help put the more abstract number work into context:

Visualising

Children often find visualising difficult and need to practise this skill. If they can see a word problem in their minds it will be easier for them to relate to it and therefore understand it and come up with a solution. It is also a useful way of introducing the vocabulary associated with problem solving, e.g. How many more? How many altogether? What is the difference?
You may need to alter the numbers depending on the age and ability of the children.

1. Close your eyes. Imagine your friend has two chocolate bars that are exactly the same. You love chocolate. Your friend offers you ³/₄ of one of the bars or ⁴/₅ of the other. *Which one are you going to choose? Why?*

2. Repeat the first question with different fractions, e.g. ⁵/₈ and ³/₄ or ⁷/₈ and ⁹/₁₀.

3. Imagine you have a piece of string that is 1m long. You need ¹/₅ to wrap a package. *What length will you have left?*

4. With the length that you have left, you are going to use ¹/₄ to make a pretend raft. *What length will you have left now?*

5. Ben has three goldfish called Wam, Bam and Sam. They love to swim around in their bowl. Imagine the goldfish in their bowl. They blow bubbles. Wam blows six bubbles, Bam blows twice as many and Sam blows four times as many. *How many bubbles are there?*

6. Bev has some goldfish. Each fish blows six bubbles and there are 120 bubbles.
   How many fish does she have?

7. There are 300 fleas jumping around on our cat. Twenty per cent of them are male.
   What number are female?

8. Imagine a clock. The time on it reads 20 minutes to five. You turn on the TV to watch your favourite programme, which starts at that time. It's just finished – your clock is slow.
   If the programme lasts for 25 minutes, what time should the clock read?

Acting out

Acting out problems is a fun way of thinking about the skills needed to solve them. It helps the children think about the information that they are being given and how to use it to work through the problem. As part of your lesson, give groups of children a short problem, some time to work out their scene and any necessary equipment, e.g. paper, pens, coins, books, Unifix cubes, plasticine – anything which will help them. During the plenary, ask them to mime their problem, using any pictures and props that they want to use. The rest of the class need to work out what the scene is all about and what the problem and its solution are.
This activity is an effective one to do with all age ranges. Below are some ideas that can be adapted to suit your particular class simply by altering the numbers.

Examples

1. Sam, Adam and Joe went to a football match. They joined the other 1570 Blues fans. There were 1525 fans watching the other team.
   How many more Blues fans were there?

A possible scenario
The group needs to have five children in it. Two of the children could each hold a large piece of paper saying 'I am a crowd of 1570 or 1525 people' (as appropriate). Three of the children could be Sam, Adam and Joe, maybe with name labels. They could walk over to the largest crowd. One of them could hold up a sign asking the question 'How many more of us than them?'
The children will probably come up with some much better ideas of their own!

2. Andrew, Katie, Fatima, Tomas and Steph have collected £26.60. They each collected the same amount.
   How much did they each collect?

3. Eric ran 5 km, George ran half that distance and Catherine ran twice as far.
   What was the difference in the distances that George and Catherine ran?

4. Mr Smith has four apple trees. On each tree there are 20 apples. Unfortunately, $\frac{1}{5}$ of the apples were eaten by maggots and were no good. The rest were edible.
   How many edible apples has Mr Smith grown altogether?

5. It was pocket money day. My mum gave my big sister twice as much as me and my little brother half as much as me.
   If my little brother was given £2.50, how much were my sister and I given?

6. Tammy and her friends went to the supermarket and bought two loaves of bread at 85p each, a big cream cake at £3.75 and eight tins of cat food at 45p each. They gave the shopkeeper a £20 note.
   How much change did they receive?

7. Raj has five dogs, 12 cats, three rabbits and 10 cockatiels. He also lives with his mum, dad, two brothers and three sisters.
   How many legs are there in his household?

8. My grandad took us on holiday in France. We left home at 7:30 am. We rode in the car for two hours to get to the ferry. The ferry journey lasted four hours. We then drove to our apartment, that took one and a quarter hours.
   At what time did we arrive?

Making up

Asking the children to make up a variety of problems from numbers or facts is a helpful way of encouraging them to think about relevant information, which operations to use and how to solve two-step problems. It enables them to put problems into a context that is meaningful to them and therefore easier for them to understand. When using this type of activity, it is essential to discuss with the children as a class the work they have done, asking such things as how they thought the problem could be solved, whether there was any redundant information and how many steps they thought were required to achieve an answer.

During a plenary on another topic, make the exercise relevant to the objectives of the lesson.

Examples

If the objective for the lesson is to 'understand that division is the inverse of multiplication', the plenary may involve writing up the numbers 120, 40, 3 and asking the children to make up some multiplication and division problems using them – including one of the numbers as the answer:

There are 40 boys in our drama group and three times as many girls.
How many are there in the group altogether?

There are 120 cakes in that box. I am going to divide them equally into those three smaller boxes.
How many will there be in each small box.

Angelo baked 120 pizzas. He packed them in equal amounts into 40 boxes to be delivered.
How many were in each box?

Esther had three football stickers; Ian had 40 times as many.
How many did Ian have?

In this case it is important to make reference to the inversion aspect from the objective during discussion of the problem work.

Other examples

Write these numbers on the board: 3124, 245, 6, 10
Give the children a few minutes to think of a problem involving those numbers.
They could work in pairs or small groups, or if you prefer individually. Pairs or small groups will give support to any who are not so confident, especially if doing this kind of activity for the first time. Discuss the problems with the class. Encourage the use of a variety of operations, e.g. group 1 make up a problem involving addition; group 2 subtraction; group 3 a mixture of multiplication and subtraction; group 4 a mixture of division and addition. This could be carried out according to ability.

Possible problems

1. There were 3124 people at the concert. It wasn't very good and half way through 245 left. Shortly after that ten went to get an ice cream and only six returned.
    How many were at the concert by the end?

    The match began at 5:30. By 5:00 there were 3124 people in the grounds. Fifteen minutes later another 245 arrived; soon after that six more people turned up. Ten people came a little later. *How many were at the match altogether?*

2.   **5kg**   **2.5kg**   **800g**
    In the pet shop there were some bags of cat food. One bag weighed 5kg, another 2.5kg and a third 800g.
    What was the total weight of the bags?
    There was 5kg of sand in my little sister's sandpit. My dad added an extra 2.5kg. My little sister took out 800g.
    How much sand is in it now?

3.   **$\frac{1}{2}$**   **20%**
    Two jumpers cost £20. In the sale one was half price and the other had 20% off.
    How much did they each cost in the sale?
    My friend and I had 1m of string each. I cut half of my piece off; my friend cut 20% of hers off.
    How much more did my friend now have?

4.   **$\frac{1}{2}$**   **58**
    There were 58 people in the restaurant. Half of them had just been to the cinema and the other half had been to the theatre.
    How many had been to the theatre?
    There were 58 birds on the field looking for worms. After a while half as many again joined them.
    How many birds were on the field then?

5.   **10:45   18**

My watch said it was 10:45. It was 18 minutes fast.
What time was it really?
At 10:45 there were 18 children in the park.
If another six children came every half an hour, how many would there be at 12:15?

6.   **187   46   54**

There were 187 pears on the pear tree. My friend picked 46 and I picked 54.
How many were left?
There were 187 people queuing to have a go on the roller-coaster; shortly afterwards another 46 joined them. Fifty-four people eventually gave up queuing and left.
How many were left in the queue?

7.   **3 hours 20 minutes   ³/₄ hour**

My family and I went to visit some friends at the seaside. We set off at 9am. It took us three hours and 20 minutes to get there. We were ³/₄ of an hour late.
At what time did our friends expect us to arrive?
Peter started his homework at 4:30. It took him 3 hours and 20 minutes to finish it. He had a break of ³/₄ of an hour at 5:30. When he had finished he had his supper.
At what time did he have his supper?

Playing games

Here are three simple games that you may find useful to have up your sleeve for the occasional plenary session. They can be adapted to use for any topic:

The Grid Game or Bingo

The idea of this game is for the children to fill in their own grids (of any size) with numbers or shapes or whatever is relevant to the lesson. You then call out types of numbers or properties of shapes. If they have any that are applicable to what you have said, they cross it out. The winner is the first player to cross out all their numbers, as in the following example.

18	27	32
~~63~~	24	~~48~~
90	80	45

Children fill their grid with numbers multiples of 8 and 9. Call out times table questions: 6 x 8, 7 x 9 etc. If the children have the answer on their grid they cross it out.

Other ideas could be:
a) Numbers from 10 to 100: ask vocabulary-based statements – multiples of 10, 5 and 2, even numbers, odd numbers, square numbers, prime numbers.
b) Any four-digit numbers: children cross out any number they have written that has the digit that you call out in the position you call it, i.e. if they have written 2856 and you say 5 in the tens or 50, they cross that out.
c) Any 2-D shapes (drawn): make statements to do with their properties, e.g. cross out all the shapes that are quadrilaterals, any that have three corners, any that have at least one right angle.

Ladders and Snakes or In the Bin

This game can also fit in with virtually any topic you might be studying. You will need a selection of around 20 cards with suitable numbers on, such as:

Weights from 0 to 1kg: write weights on the cards, using grams and decimals, i.e. 350g, 0.4kg. Pick the cards randomly. As each one is drawn, call it out. The children need to write it in a rectangle of the ladder. The aim is to fill up the ladder with numbers ordered from lowest at the bottom to highest at the top. Any that won't fit go into the snake. For example:

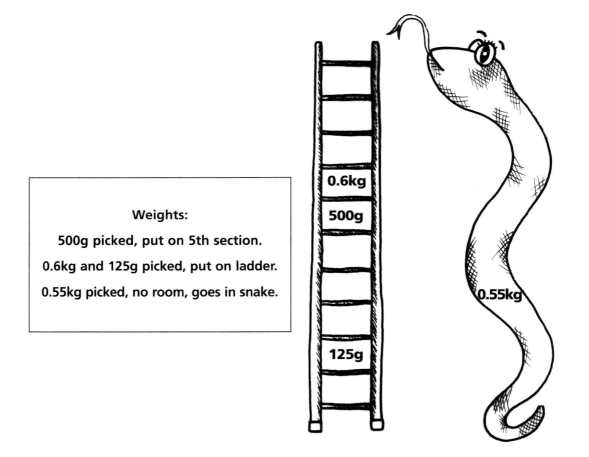

Weights:

500g picked, put on 5th section.

0.6kg and 125g picked, put on ladder.

0.55kg picked, no room, goes in snake.

There is a blank snake and ladder grid on photocopiable sheet 15.

Play Your Cards Right

Great fun! This game follows similar rules to the television game show. It allows for much questioning and it is important to do plenty of this to make the most of the game. You will need to make about 20 cards with numbers on to do with a particular topic, e.g. multiples of 6 or fractions, decimals and percentages which are excellent for this. The children need to predict whether the next card will be higher or lower than the preceding number. They need to predict five in a row correctly. The class could play as a whole group; however, it can be more exciting if you divide them into two teams.

Example

Cards between 0 and 1 for fractions, decimals and percentages

50	$\frac{1}{5}$	**0.6**	**15**
0.5	$\frac{7}{10}$	**20**	$\frac{1}{4}$

First card:

15

Q: Predict whether the next card will be higher or lower.
A: 'Higher'
Q: Why do you think that?

Second card:

$\frac{7}{10}$

Q: What is the difference between this card and the previous one?
A: 55%
Q: How did you work that out?

Third card:

$\frac{1}{4}$

Q: Were you right to go lower?
A: Yes.
Q: How much lower is this card?
A: 45%
Q: What about the next card?
A: Higher
Q: Why?

Fourth card:

20

Q: Are you right
A: No.
Q: Why? Whoops! Try again.

Photocopiable Sheet 15
Snake and ladder

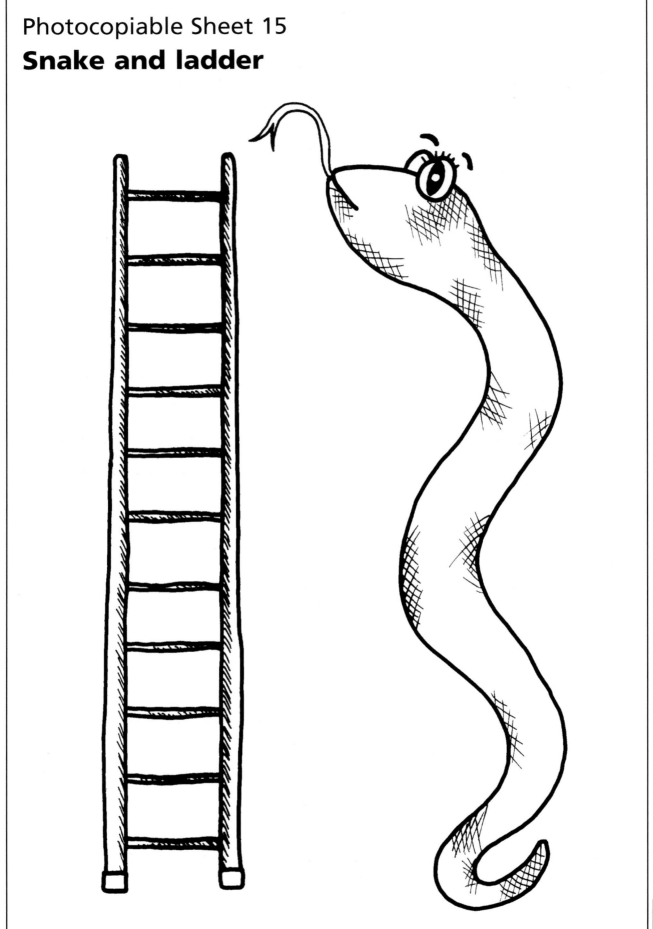

Chapter 5
Other ideas for an effective plenary
Analysing the lesson

Ask the children what they found easy about the lesson and why. Do the same thing with the other two aspects. Focus on one of them during one plenary and another, another time.

1. Record their comments on the 'easy' parts as if brainstorming.

Year 6 example

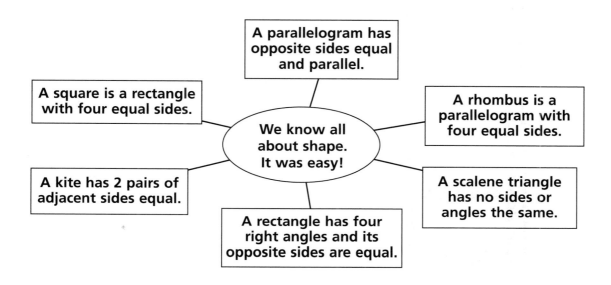

2. Have a vote to find out which was the most enjoyable part of the lesson and why. Use that information to build a bar graph with the class:

Year 5 example
Ratio paint blots

Children's comments: "I enjoyed the whole lesson." So did five others.
"I enjoyed working with a group." So did six others.
"I enjoyed guessing and ordering the other groups ratios."
So did eight others.
"I enjoyed mixing the paints and making blobs." So did 11 others.

Invite some children to come to the board to construct the graph and add the labels.

3. Make a display of one of the children's favourite parts of the lesson; this can be used later as a prompt when the subject next comes up.

Year 6 example
Angles

Make some statements on card or paper and invite a few children to match them with appropriate pictures and draw on the positions of the angles with a curve or half box as appropriate:

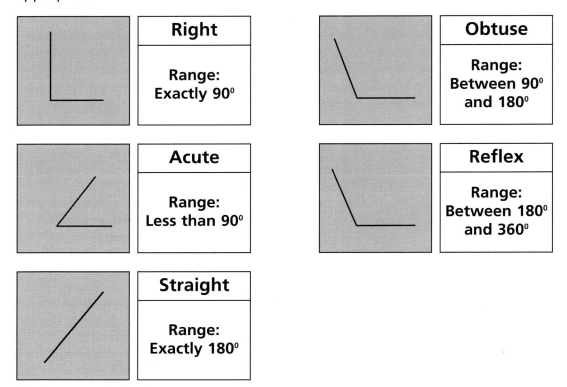

4. Discuss the most difficult part of the lesson. Find out what made it so and where the children have a particular problem. This is not the occasion to try to sort out any problems as it may well take more time than is available, but make a note so that you can work on them again the next day or whenever is most appropriate. Make a poster to show who has a difficulty and with what – only do this if there is a large group of children with the same feeling and follow that up with another when they have succeeded.

Year 5 example

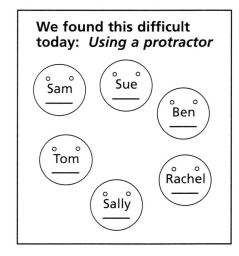

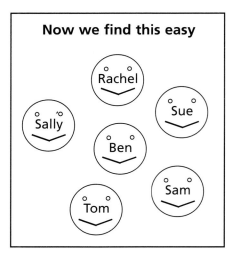

Identifying misconceptions

The above ideas help to identify any misconceptions that have occurred. If these are minor ones that can easily be sorted out, deal with them during the plenary. If they are more complicated, make a note of them and deal with them next time you meet for maths. However, if you notice during individual, paired or group work that there is a problem or misconception most of the class are having, or common errors are being made, stop the lesson and go straight into a 'plenary' for the rest of the session in order to sort it out.

Making general rules

Children should be helped to generalise a rule from examples generated by different groups.

Examples
1. A number is always divisible by 9 if the sum of its digits is divisible by 9.
2. To multiply by 25, multiply by 100 and then halve and halve again.
3. The number of lines of symmetry in a regular polygon is equal to the number of sides.
4. The sum of three odd numbers is always odd.
5. An odd number can be written as twice a number plus one, e.g. 35 is twice 17 plus 1.
6. A prime number can only be divided by one and itself.

Reflection

You can use this to draw together what has been learned, reflect on what was important in the lesson, and summarise key facts, ideas and vocabulary and what needs to be remembered. This needs to be discussion based. There should be lots of interaction with the children, asking them appropriate questions, listening to them talking about their work and discussing what they think is the important aspect to remember. Summarising key facts, ideas and objectives is an important part of this type of plenary, as is the reviewing of the vocabulary that the children should have learnt.

Drawing it together

This needs to be a discussion-based session. Once again, there should be lots of interaction with the children, asking appropriate questions and listening to them talking about their work. At the end of a unit it is important to draw together what has been learnt over the series of lessons by summarising key facts, ideas and objectives.

Celebrate success in the children's work

Discuss with the children whether they think they have been successful during their group or whole-class work in achieving the objective of the lesson. Ask for comments as to why they think they have succeeded and ask them to give an example of the work they have completed. Then try one of the following:

1. Invite other children to say something positive to the child, pair or group about their particular success.
2. Give the child/pair/group a clap.
3. Have a success poster or sheet on the wall and write that success and the children's names beside it, for example:

This week we are learning to find percentages.

Peter, David and Jo know how to find 15% of an amount by finding 10% and halving it for 5% and adding the two.

Katie and Abu know how to find 25% by finding 50% and halving it.

Add to this over the week and continue with it next time the topic is revisited, so that every child will see their name on the chart over a period of time. Add any small success; this is particularly important for those children who lack confidence.

4. Award points or merits for success, maybe display them on a poster, e.g.

We have succeeded!

Ben

Adam

Maggie

5. At the end of a topic, if the children have worked well and achieved success have a celebration 'party', playing lots of maths games and having a drink and biscuit. Create a special plenary by inviting other children or the head of the school along to share these successes with them.

Number cards A

1	**2**	**3**
4	**5**	**6**
7	**8**	**9**
10	**11**	**12**
13	**14**	**15**

Number cards B

16	**17**	**18**
19	**20**	**21**
22	**23**	**24**
25	**26**	**27**
28	**29**	**30**